Celebrating a Centenary

Teacher Education at Sheffield Hallam University

Bruce Collins
Ruth Morgan

The material for this book is drawn from a range of sources, including original documents, official publications, and books and articles. The format of the book is designed for ready accessibility and does not have a scholarly framework of references. The book offers a synthesis of material from the institution's history and ideas and research within the field. It is not intended as an original scholarly contribution. The sources used are cited in the References and Further Reading.

ISBN No. 1 84387 155 6

Published by	Sheffield Hallam University
	Faculty of Development and Society
Design and typesetting	Dawn Williams Design Studio Department of Marketing
Print	Slater Print Group

© Sheffield Hallam University 2005

Whilst every effort has been made to ensure that the information contained in this publication is accurate and up-to-date, neither the authors nor publisher can accept legal responsibility or liability for anything done by readers in consequence of any errors or omissions.

All rights reserved. No part of the publication may be reproduced, stored in a retrieval system or transmitted in any form or by any means mechanical, electronic, photocopying, recording or otherwise, without the prior written permission of the publishers.

The information in this publication can be made available in alternative formats. Please contact us on 0114 225 5555 for details.

Acknowledgements

We would like to thank the many people who have helped us research and write this book. We thank Sylvia Johnson and Angela Rees for starting and co-ordinating the Centenary project of which this was a part. Many Sheffield Hallam University staff have helped us, from Facilities staff in Estates and Security, Marketing staff, including Dale Martin, Jenna Hollingsworth and Dawn Shepherd, for support in many ways, with publicity, arranging meetings, scanning photos and many other ways, and in particular Dawn Williams for her patience and design skills in setting out the text and illustrations.

We thank former students Roy Millington, who wrote the 1955 Jubilee history of the College on which we drew heavily, and Geoff Warburton and other members of the Crescenters alumni organisation who have been so helpful and informative.

We thank those who have come in to talk to us or in other ways shared their memories of life at City College with us

- former students Judith Rossiter, Norah Armfield, Wendy Green, Shirley Payne, Sue Holmes, John and Robert Driskell, Decalie Baldwin, among others
- former staff Brian Carlson, Bernard Jones, Paul Cutts, Mabel Leather, John Salt, Constance Gilbey, Shirley Payne, Peter Downey, David Bradshaw
- current staff Mike Holland, Stuart Trickey, Robin Smith, Ian Dall, Sue Bamford, Paul Dickinson, Tricia Young and others

The staff of Sheffield Archives and Local Studies Library have been immensely helpful in locating documents. Others have guided us through the local history, including Nyra Wilson, and members of the Broomhall Park Residents' Association, in particular archivist Jim Fox and Barry Cummings. The General Teaching Council has been very helpful in extracting data for us on the local teaching profession.

The illustrations are sourced as follows

- most colour photographs of the campus today were taken by one of the authors (RM); a small number come from the Sheffield Hallam University collection
- we thank the Crescenters for allowing us to use many images from their archive, on pages 27-29, 33-35, 50-53, 56-58, 62, 64, 65, 74, 78, 81, 83, 84, 94, 98, 99, 101, 112 and 113
- the set of photos of the Principals as younger men on pages 78-80 are reproduced thanks to Roy Millington
- the Sheffield Local Studies Library collection of old photographs (Picture.Sheffield) provided the images on pages 18, 22, 23, 26, 32, 73, 76, 100, 105, 109 and 112, reproduced by kind permission of the Head of Culture, Sheffield City Council
- items from books, sale plans and maps in the Local Studies collection, on pages 17-20, 35, 37, 38, 56, 57, 63, 73, 77, 80, 92, 93, 95, 96, 100, 103, 104, 106-108 and 113, are also reproduced by kind permission of the Head of Culture, Sheffield City Council
- we thank Alan Godfrey Maps for allowing us to reproduce a section of the 1905 Old OS Map of the Collegiate area on page 21
- Judith Rossiter supplied the photos of the 1976 occupation on pages 63 and 103
- We thank Mabel Fradley (nee Leather) for the photograph of herself as a young woman on page 82
- Neville Denson allowed us to reproduce his illustration of the Will's cigarette card of Stainless Stephen on page 75, originally published in The Dalesman in February 2000
- Thanks go to the National Portrait Gallery, London, for the photograph of the portrait of William Brookfield on page 72
- The photo of Bruce Oldfield in his student days, on page 85, comes from his autobiography *'Rootless'* and we thank Random House for permission to reproduce it

Staff and some secondary teacher training graduates, City Campus, 2005

Contents

Introduction — 9

The first fifty years — 11
Collegiate School and Grammar School — 18
White's map of 1885 — 20
Area of Collegiate Campus, 1905 — 21
World War One — 22
Collegiate Campus buildings, 1905 — 24
Collegiate Campus buildings, 1911 — 25
Sport — 26
Garden parties — 29
World War Two — 30
Accommodation — 32

Growth and merger — 39
Collegiate Campus buildings, 1950 — 49
School practice — 50
Libraries — 52
Academic staffing — 54
The College identity — 56
Food — 58
Money — 60
Curriculum — 61
Student life — 62
Drama — 64

Academic developments in the 1980s — 67
William Brookfield — 72
Sir William Christopher Leng — 73
Annie Jennings (Thomas) — 74
Stainless Stephen — 75
Music and Sir Henry Coward — 76
College Principals — 78
Mabel Leather and support staff — 82
Alderman Marshall, JP — 84
Bruce Oldfield — 85
Collegiate Campus buildings, 1970 — 86

Re-alignments   87
Southbourne   92
Parkholme   95
Oaklands   96
Collegiate Hall   100
College House, formerly Oakdale   103
Broomgrove Road houses   104
Mundella, formerly Belmont   107
Main Building   108

Recent trends   115
Student numbers and key events, 1905-2005   124
Teacher training graduates, 2005   126
Collegiate Campus buildings, 2005   128

Conclusions   129

References and further reading   135

Glossary   138

Introduction

The Education Act of 1902 substantially advanced the state's role in the provision of education. As one outcome from that act, local authorities set up residential teacher training colleges to meet unprecedented demands for qualified teachers. Sheffield City Training College, formally opened on 13 October 1905, was only the second one to be established. Ever since then, teacher education has been provided at the Collegiate site of what is now Sheffield Hallam University. Given this long and continuous record of achievement, it seems appropriate that we should celebrate the College's centenary.

This is most definitely not an official history. The Victorians used to write what were pejoratively called 'tombstone biographies' of great worthies. Even today reviewers occasionally refer to major tomes as 'definitive histories'. This book does not provide a lavishly embellished and reverentially phrased memorial to a century of activity. Nor does it attempt to recapture the full range of professional experiences lived by those who taught and studied Education, or the often passionately felt and expressed ideas about teacher education that those engaged in it articulated.

Our work has two objectives. First, we seek to recapture aspects of the history of Education at the Collegiate site which are likely to be unfamiliar to present-day readers. We have selected a wide range of specific topics and unusual - certainly atypical - individuals and provided short sections on them. The approach is highly selective but aims to convey the variety of staff's and students' life and work, particularly in the first sixty years of teacher education at Collegiate. Roy Millington in 1955 wrote a good history of the College's first half-century. We have been able to summarise those years briefly because he has provided an effective account of that period. But he had only a limited opportunity to illustrate the text, whereas we have used the centenary as a welcome opportunity to disseminate a fuller range of visual material. A vital part of the College's development was its steady acquisition of additional buildings on the Collegiate site. We have compiled separate entries for many of the more interesting older buildings to demonstrate their varied ownership and use, and the importance of many of them to upper-middle class life in the city from the 1840s to the 1930s.

The second objective is to analyse and reflect upon some of the main themes and issues concerning the development and, possibly, the future of teacher education. Because so many elements of Education provision within an institution - notably the curriculum and the numbers of student teachers recruited - flow from national initiatives and policies, any history of the fortunes of Education within the College/Polytechnic/University depends upon an understanding of the periodic and sometimes radical shifts in the requirements laid down by government and its agencies. The discussion here interweaves an account of national developments in teacher education with a history of the main issues facing Education in the College/Polytechnic/University. It is hoped that this may be of interest and value to past, present and future staff and students who seek an understanding of the policy contexts in which teacher education has unfolded and will evolve.

The views expressed on these issues and the selection of topics and material for the book are entirely our responsibility. They do not reflect any official position or policy on the part of the Division of Education and Humanities, the Faculty of Development and Society, or Sheffield Hallam University.

We held interviews with many past and current members of staff and former students. These are acknowledged separately. It is always invidious to single out individuals, but it would also be wrong not to give separate thanks to three participants. Roy Millington and John Salt, who held senior academic management posts in the Polytechnic in the 1970s and 1980s, both provided us with incisive and stimulating insights and suggestions on detailed decisions and general developments alike. We have not had the space or time to follow up all their stimulating leads. But they have contributed to the formulation of a possible research project for the future involving both the process of decision-making and the College's social history. David Bradshaw, Deputy Principal in 1968-1970 and later Principal of Doncaster College, provided measured and thoroughly thought-out analyses of both national and local developments, which clarified a number of contentious issues.

Mentioning interviews with individuals raises an important point about the book. We have gained from past and present staff and students an invaluable insight into working life at Collegiate, and have been able to provide selective material on the experiences of former staff and students. But chapters of the book focus on policy and development over time. We recognise that this focus does not capture many of the challenges and controversies and much of the bustle and grind of everyday work in Education: the curriculum designed, re-designed, amended, re-amended; teaching strategies devised, reviewed, revised, renewed; learning materials sorted, white-boarded, Black-boarded, Power-Pointed; students encouraged, enthused, enlightened, evaluated. Nor does it do justice to the importance of personal interactions and external working partnerships throughout the process of teacher education. It provides instead a set of reflections upon the context in which all this activity takes place.

Sheffield Hallam University is a strong national provider of Initial Teacher Training, which is the main focus of this book. The University is one of the largest providers of ITT in the country. It is committed to delivering training in the secondary shortage subjects and to providing trainees with the maximum possible choice of routes through professional training. The 5,914 teachers who gained Qualified Teacher Status from the University in the years 1994 to 2004 inclusive, represent a huge infusion of skill, enthusiasm and commitment, all honed by often demanding application as trainees. Recent Ofsted inspections attest to consistently good quality provision and yield sound ratings across primary and secondary training and what is a necessarily complex variety of routes. Students record high levels of satisfaction with the teaching and personal support they receive and the courses they undertake. But all these strong and positive indicators do not guarantee stability or success in the future. This short history seeks to offer a framework for understanding how past policies have shaped the development of teacher education and how powerful challenges concerning the scale and shape of teacher education have occurred, occur now, and will continue to occur in the future.

Bruce Collins
Ruth Morgan

13 October 2005

The first fifty years

Teacher education at the Collegiate site resulted from national developments and local initiatives. National public concern at the lack of proper training for school teachers grew from the 1880s. In 1902 only 40 per cent of elementary teachers in England had formal certification and elementary teachers formed the vast bulk of the teaching work force. Pressure for reform flowed from arguments that English education was suffering from falling standards and that the British economy was being challenged by the superior technological skills and industrial competitiveness of Germany and the USA. The political response to these concerns was to give local authorities control over schools and teacher training and, in 1906, to make central government funding available for up to 75 per cent of the capital costs of providing training colleges.

While most local authorities failed to take up the teacher training challenge, Sheffield City Council reacted promptly. The Education Committee set up in 1903 ensured that teacher training formed part of a strategic realignment of secondary education in the city. Sheffield Royal Grammar School had been moved to the Collegiate Crescent site in the mid-1830s as part of a long-term plan by the local landowner to develop his farmlands as an upper-middle class and gated residential area. In 1903 the city council decided to merge the school, based in what is now Main Building and the central part of Collegiate Hall, with Wesley College and consolidate the new King Edward VII School on Wesley College's site. The city purchased the Collegiate Crescent premises of the old grammar school to form the nucleus of a new training college. At the same time, the University College, which became the University of Sheffield also in 1905, needed to off-load its responsibilities for the small Day Training College for teachers. Provision at the Day Training College was formally judged to be incompatible with university-level work. So, the new training college started life with 90 new entrants and 42 transferees from the old Day Training College.

The founding of the new college owed a great deal to a curious mix of commendable local initiative and necessary short-term fixes. The fact that an important programme to improve the professional quality of elementary school teaching would be undertaken in buildings designed for a small grammar school set in an affluent, gated residential area proved to be characteristic of much government provision for teacher education in the Twentieth-century. Spare buildings across the country were regularly enlisted as training colleges. Also typical of a mind-set was the appointment of The Reverend Valentine Ward Pearson as the first principal (1905-1921). Pearson had been headmaster of Wesley College for thirteen years. While his Methodism may have suited the denominational leanings of many city fathers, he knew nothing of teacher training and appears to have had no pronounced scholarly or academic interests. His appointment arose from the merger of his school.

On the other hand, the new college went against the trend set by the Nineteenth-century denominational training colleges and admitted both men and women. Few of the new local education authority colleges did that. Yet the extent of innovation was limited. Once Southbourne was purchased and greatly extended (by 1911), men and women students lived at opposite ends of the Collegiate 'site'. They were not taught in the same classrooms and lecture rooms until the 1930s. Regulations and disciplinary measures aimed to minimise their social contacts.

Allowing for such contradictions, Sheffield was at the forefront of the development of training colleges. It was the second local authority to establish a college and even by 1914 only 20 out of 146 authorities had followed the lead. Much effort went into ensuring that facilities were adequate. Using capital funding from central government, it bought the Brookfields' house - Southbourne - on Clarkehouse Road and completed extensive additions, providing teaching rooms, library, dining room, kitchens and study-bedrooms for 60 male students by 1911. Collegiate Hall was also greatly extended by that date. Early difficulties with the provision of science laboratories were overcome. The substantial advance made in supporting teacher training was then disrupted by World War One when the College was used as a military hospital. About 64,000 troops were treated or convalesced at the College during the years 1914-1919. Thus, in the first fourteen years of its history, the College operated for the purposes for which it was established and with the facilities deemed appropriate for its functions only during the three years 1911-1914.

The early years of the College cast occasional light on a debate which recurs throughout the history of teacher training. At the formal opening ceremony on 13 October 1905, Sir William Anson, the junior Minister for Education, argued that the College's main task was to train its students to teach. Although a liberal-minded Conservative and an Oxford academic, Anson offered a narrow interpretation of the training colleges' role which remains a politically influential model. An alternative view was suggested in October,1911, when Earl Loreburn, the Liberal Lord Chancellor, formally opened Southbourne and the Collegiate Hall extensions. From the reformist wing of the party, Loreburn asserted the importance of life-long learning and the enduring nature of learning acquired by individuals themselves. If teachers were to inspire in others the pursuit of life-long learning, they needed to be encouraged and enabled to extend their own learning. While there have been far more radical ideas about the nature of teacher training, the essential alternatives offered by policy-makers in this field were clearly expressed in the College's earliest years.

For the most part, the College concentrated on training and maintaining a strictly defined life-style among the students. The two inter-war decades were the most stable in the College's history. Following a recovery and then growth in numbers of students after 1920, the College acquired Oaklands, a large private house, in 1930 for student accommodation, but otherwise expanded little. Student numbers reached 230 in the early 1930s but fell in the second half of the decade. As the birth rate fell with the onset and continuation of the economic depression, there was limited prospect of returning to earlier levels of student population. Accommodation available in the 1930s provided for 90 men and 115 women students with few non-residents. When the College was founded, one reason for local authorities' reluctance to establish training colleges was the fear of other authorities' schools 'poaching' students trained at the host authorities' expense. But most students were home-grown. Of the college's first intake of 90 in 1905, nearly half came from the city of Sheffield and over one-third came from the West Riding. By the early 1930s the LEA ensured that candidates from Sheffield had preference for admission and the HMI report of 1936 noted that the Principal's power to reject candidates was more constrained than usual and that entrants' academic qualifications were lower *'than is customary'*. Of the 100 entrants in 1935, equally divided between men and women, just over half came from Sheffield.

The inspection report of 1935 indicated general satisfaction with the subject teaching while drawing attention to major defects in support provision. The more notable criticisms of teaching focused on physical education. There were interesting issues around the lack of relationship between academic work and practical teaching in mathematics, and around the heavy emphasis in French on literature, at the expense of the study of French contemporary civilisation and the spoken language. But the report stressed the weight given by the College to students' professional training, with the time allotted to it being *'probably more than in most Colleges'*. The main defect in resources concerned the gymnasium, and this was replaced by a new one, still in use, in 1938. There was evidence of perhaps excessive penny-pinching. At Southbourne, the sheets in study-bedrooms were changed only once a fortnight and the kitchens needed upgrading. In Collegiate Hall, the women's residence, *'The cost of food per student is at present so low as to suggest that economy in the supply is being carried to undesirable lengths.'*

World War Two caused far less general upheaval for the College than World War One had produced. But postwar developments started a new period of growth. The school leaving age was raised to 15, leading to immediate demands for more secondary teachers, the majority of whom were male. Returning non-graduate servicemen were given one year's training, instead of the required two, and then inspected on the first years of their teaching in school before becoming formally qualified. This demand for secondary teachers and the special circumstances created by returning servicemen led to the College having more men than women students for a brief phase of its history. Student numbers nearly doubled from 1940 to 1950.

Following this spurt of expansion in the 1940s, the College focused in the early 1950s on internal change under Dr. Herbert Wing (1949-1965) and his deputy, Jane Moulton (1948-1967). Significant advances were made in student representation and in involving students in running their own affairs. For the first time since its founding, the College began to function fully as a single social entity rather than forming two, although increasingly interacting, male and female enclaves. Yet, despite the importance of such attitudinal shifts, they occurred within a relatively stable microcosm. Student numbers had, after all, grown only from 189 in 1910 to 349 in 1955, and the number and scale of the buildings had not altered greatly since 1911. The demands and adjustments of the decade after 1945 represented a mild prelude to the turbulence that lay ahead.

The fiftieth anniversary of the College's founding coincided with the issuance of the report of an HMI inspection, the first since 1935-1936. It was a difficult review. On the one hand, Herbert Wing had done much to renew the lecturing staff, to emphasise academic standards in teaching, and to ease up on many of the College's tighter regulations. But his relatively liberal approach to curriculum design created difficulties of its own. For example, the inspectors found the programme in Principles and Practices of Education heavily overloaded, *'the overload is, more than anything, a testimony to the Principal's wholehearted attempt to give all members of the Education Team as much freedom as he can and to their response to it'*. A repeated concern of the report was that very thorough lecturing and well-prepared teaching materials left students with limited time for independent reading and little incentive to engage in such reading. For example, despite the efforts and academic ability of the history lecturer, the students in the Ordinary level course did not read independently or see the point of doing so. In English the lecturing staff were so well-organised and so proficient that the students *'suffer, it seems, quite literally, from too much of a good thing. Too large a proportion of their time is spent in listening and taking notes and too small a proportion in reading, thinking, discussing and in committing their own thoughts to paper.'* They were *'treated too much like grammar school boys and girls and too little like university undergraduates'*, with a predictably adverse effect on their intellectual maturation. For most subjects, the inspectors noted much to praise, as well as reservations, often about resources. Only rarely did they criticise the lack of coherence in a subject's curriculum.

The key problem raised by the inspection was what might be termed the 'British disease' of the 1940s and 1950s, familiar to economic historians. Old equipment, old facilities, old buildings were simply expected and required to keep chugging along, bearing the strains of steadily increasing demand without being sufficiently repaired, replenished or replaced. The report of 1954 repeatedly returned to the point that College facilities, provided essentially for the 186 students enrolled each year in 1936-1938 were coping with nearly double that number (349) by 1954-1955 without any significant increase in resources. Library stocks were inadequate and, in some areas, out of date. Science teaching facilities were *'no longer adequate for the needs of the College'*. A similar judgement flowed from the heavily increased pressure on student accommodation. Nearly 80 per cent of students were in residence. Collegiate Hall provided cubicles - each seven feet by ten feet - for 123 women students in eight dormitories. They had not been improved for 20 years and the furniture was *'somewhat shabby and scanty'*. Partitions between the cubicles did not reach the ceilings and the only way of reading after lights out, according to one former student, was by draping items of clothing over the tops of lamp shades. Southbourne accommodated 64 men, but again had scarcely been improved since the mid 1930s and afforded little personal privacy. Another 36 first-year men students lived in 9 and 11 Broomgrove Road, where *'there is no individual privacy at all. Some rooms are shared by four or five men with little space between the beds'*. All the basic facilities were *'inadequate or inconvenient'* and there was no telephone in the two houses. Although conditions were better in Oaklands, the former private house provided accommodation for an academic and his wife acting as warden and assistant matron plus 20 men students who had *'no individual privacy at all'*. Given these limitations, the HMIs' conclusion was unsurprising, *'The College has considerable facilities as a training unit, but it is clear that major reconstructions of the existing premises, plus some substantial new buildings, are required if this is to become a compact, efficient, economic and well organised College.'* Efforts to keep up-to-date and thorough teaching were undermined by *'inadequate, insufficient and unsuitable accommodation'*.

The timing of these recommendations could scarcely have been more awkward for the city council. The local authority's capital budget for Education was heavily committed to completing the first phase and erecting the second phase of the superstructure of the College of Technology at Pond Street. In total, its two phases of building works for the Colleges of Technology and Commerce were planned to absorb £628,170 over a number of years. Despite that massive existing financial commitment, the HMI report clearly set the agenda for a major programme of new building and the acquisition of new buildings which occurred from the late 1950s, with three new halls of residence being opened in 1961-1962: Marshall (named after Alderman Samuel Hartley Marshall), Woodville and Broomgrove.

Life in the College involved working very closely together within a closed community in conditions of considerable austerity. Ironically for an institution which appeared traditional in many aspects, 80 per cent of the academic staff in 1954 had been appointed since 1946 and only two of the total academic staff of 29, including the Principal and Deputy Principal, had been at the College for more than 15 years. Some ex-students have suggested that most pre-war staff lacked strong academic commitments and that Wing in particular made an important impact through the calibre of his appointments to lecturing posts. Despite such a focus on academic aspects of teaching, lecturers were heavily committed to pastoral duties. No fewer than 13 of the 29 academic staff lived in College and held responsibilities relating to students' residential life. But living quarters for tutors and their tutorial rooms were inadequate. The Principal's house was in the central section of Southbourne and the Principal acted as warden for that residence. He and his family had limited private life in the midst of their involvement with the students. Not surprisingly, given this cheek-by-jowl existence, the inspectors found that, *'The staff as a whole work under strain and at times there appears to be some nervous tension amongst them.'* Wing himself suffered from a nervous collapse in 1954, and his deputy, Jane Moulton, who took up her post in 1948, carried a considerable administrative load, eventually retiring in 1967.

Close staff-student contact began with the interview for admission. Interviews were conducted by the Principal, Deputy Principal, and an official from the Sheffield LEA, sometimes followed by an interview with tutorial staff and a written test. In 1954 there were three applicants per place with about 15 per cent more applicants giving the College as their first choice than there were places. The majority of students came from Sheffield and its near region. Very few students came from southern England. The students' geographical origins thus provided a significant element of cohesion. Further cohesion was provided by the pattern of teaching and social life. Students were required to attend all classes, which ran from 9.00am to 5.00pm on weekdays and on Saturday morning. The intensity of the timetable left little time for reflection or discussion. In addition, the College sustained 15 societies and committees focusing on students' interests and needs. Although the physical facilities were described as inadequate and the living environment was austere and afforded little privacy to the students, their lives were extremely busy, thoroughly planned, and subject to close supervision by the tutorial staff.

The academic load for the two years of study pursued by the students was extremely heavy. All students took Principles and Practice of Education and Health Education and basic courses in five subjects: physical education, English and (in the first year only) mathematics, art, and religious knowledge. Throughout their two years students also studied two subjects, one to an advanced level. Thus in their first year students studied up to ten different subjects, and second-year students took up to seven. In 1954-1955 the 178 students in their second year took advanced options as indicated in the table on page 16.

The pattern of specialist study shows that only 12 of the 178 second-year students chose general sciences or physics or chemistry. Of the 106 women students, only eight took any science or mathematics at advanced level; 41 of them took English, history or geography; and 33 took art, craft or dresscraft. The striking lack of students engaged in the advanced study of mathematics and the sciences other than biology was compounded by the poor state of the science teaching laboratories. Even with such small numbers the resources were deemed inadequate by the HMIs.

More generally, the total number of students taking both the advanced and ordinary courses underscored the atomised nature of specialist study. Few subjects could sustain more that two specialist tutors and many could sustain only one. That left them very exposed to staff illness and very dependent upon the range of knowledge and pedagogic skills of only one or two lecturers in any one subject. It is perhaps not surprising to find the attitude which greeted one College trainee when he got a teaching post at the College of Commerce; since he was a qualified teacher, he was expected to teach anything, wherever a timetable gap appeared.

1954-1955 student second-year options

	Advanced level only	(of whom men)	Total of Advanced and Ordinary levels
Geography	38	16	59
Craft	19	6	46
Physical education	18	7	32
English	17	5	48
History	16	9	22
Biology	13	8	32
Art	13	4	24
Dresscraft	11	-	17
Religious knowledge	9	3	19
Music	7	1	14
Mathematics	5	4	22
Chemistry	4	3	4
Physics	3	3	3
Handicraft	3	3	10
General sciences	2	1	5

The structural dangers inherent in this syllabus are obvious. Students got little time to probe any subject deeply or to acquire an extensive knowledge of it. The case for a three-year course of study, made in the McNair report of 1944, seems compelling. The lack of mathematics and science expertise among the trainees was also ominous for school teaching in the future. The dominance of geography seems curious to us today, as does the lack of synergy between geography and those mathematical and scientific skills which are central to so many of its practical applications. Equally ominous for the future was the total absence of any options in modern foreign languages. The tutors' commitment to teaching and the thoroughness of that teaching were commended by the inspectorate. But at its first half century point, the College's syllabus demonstrated why so much about the focus of British teacher education remained open to debate.

Collegiate School and Grammar School

Until the 1840s, the area consisted of fields belonging to the Broomhall Park Estate and Broomgrove farm (see Fairbanks' 1795 map), gently sloping down to the Porter Brook, with names such as Nether Meadow and Briery Holme. Ecclesall Road was a new toll road, which opened in 1812.

The Collegiate School's foundation goes back to 1603 in premises near Campo Lane, followed by the building of a new school in 1823 in Broad Lane, but this did not meet the requirements of the local gentry. In 1834, it was agreed by church members to found Sheffield Proprietary School with a committee of shareholders and twelve trustees belonging to the Church of England. Shares were on offer up to a maximum 120 at £25 each, and 112 were bought by 95 gentlemen. Scholars were to be nominated by the shareholders. Lord Wharncliffe, lord of the manor of Wortley, was elected President of the Management Committee, with the Vicar of Sheffield, The Reverend J Sutton, as Vice-President. He was later followed by The Reverend Thomas Sale (who lived in 34 Collegiate Crescent in the 1850s).

COLLEGIATE SCHOOL.

In November 1834, 2.2 acres of land on the Broomhall Park Estate were bought from the landowner, a solicitor John Watson, for £1,035, with a further acre added in 1836 for £917, on *'a beautiful and healthy site, about one mile distant from the town on the Derbyshire side'* (Hunter 1870s). The school authority funded half the access from Ecclesall Road, while Watson laid out Collegiate Crescent, extended Broomhall Road and improved Park Lane, adding the lodge gates at each entrance.

On 26 September 1835 Lord Wharncliffe laid the first stone of a fine single-storey Gothic school building (now known as Main Building) designed by John Grey Weightman (1801-1872), later a partner of ME Hadfield, a practice on Broomgrove Road with long associations with the College. The school building cost £10,000 to build and accommodated 120 pupils. It consisted of a central hall with large windows, two classrooms flanking each side and walled outdoor exercise space behind. The school was to provide a *'sound and liberal education'*... to enable boys to *'proceed to universities or enter directly upon a*

Detail from Fairbanks map, 1795

professional or business career' (*Collegiate Magazine* 1852). Two lines of education could be followed, classical leading to university or commercial leading to a mercantile profession.

The Collegiate School opened on 1 August 1836. The teachers and 40 of the pupils lived in the plainer, Tudor-style Headmaster's house which opened in 1837 and which may also have been designed by Weightman; it is now the central part of Collegiate Hall on Ecclesall Road.

Grammar School in the 1880s

An early pupil was the scientist Henry Clifton Sorby who lived in the area of Woodbourne, Attercliffe; he attended the school up to the age of 15 in 1841. Many pupils came from families living on the Victorian Broomhall Park Estate and the presence of the school was an attraction to living in the area.

Henry Wilson (owner of Westbrook Snuff Mill) came forward in 1852 with financial help to appoint new masters when the head resigned, and he ran the school for three years out of his own pocket; again in 1871 he saved the school from closure by buying the property.

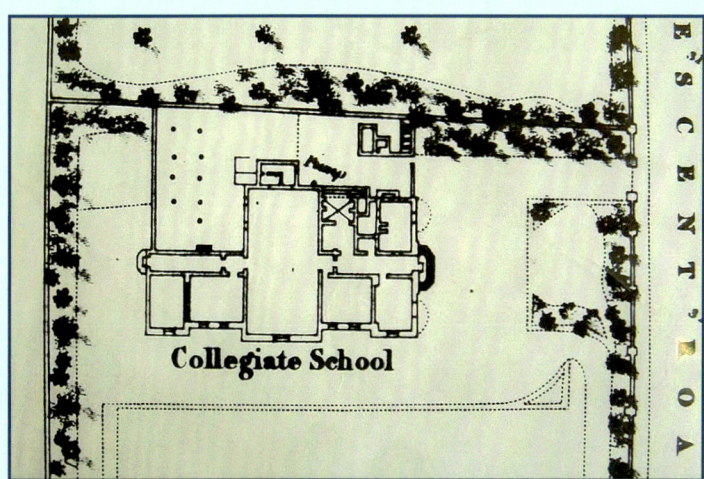

Map of Collegiate School, 1853

In 1885 the school merged with the grammar school in St George's Square and became Sheffield Grammar School. Additional rooms were added to the west end of the building. It continued until the 1902 Education Act resolved to strengthen secondary education and in 1905 it merged with the Wesley College and became King Edward VII School. This freed up buildings and land for a teacher training college.

White's map of 1855

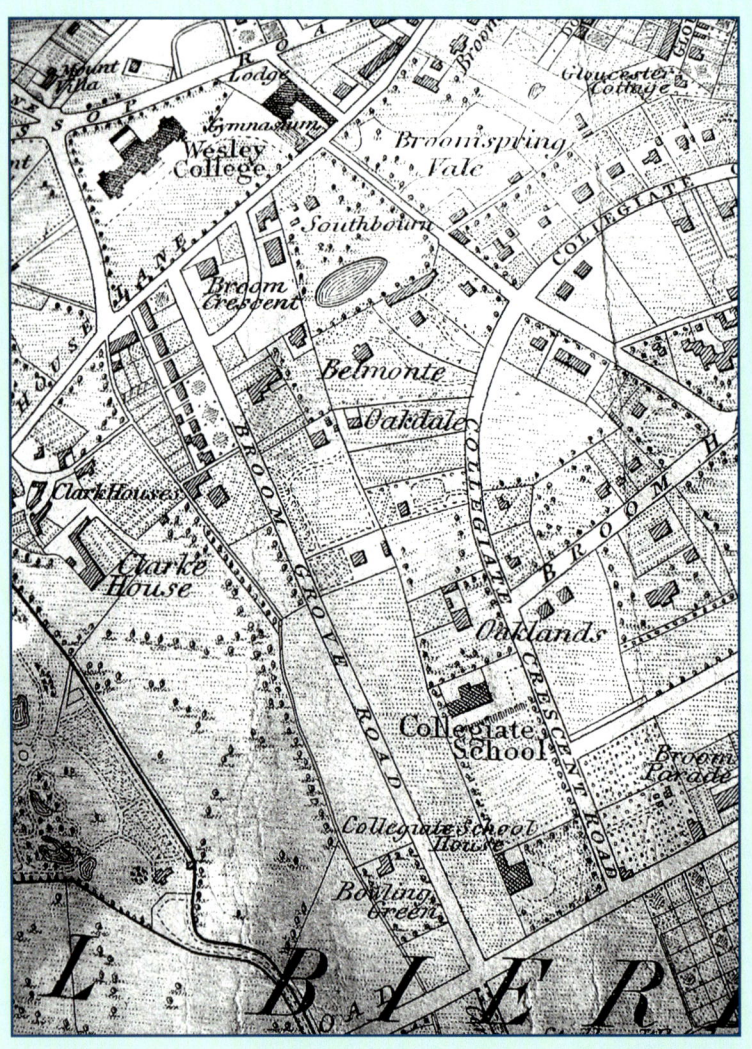

Area of Collegiate Campus, 1905

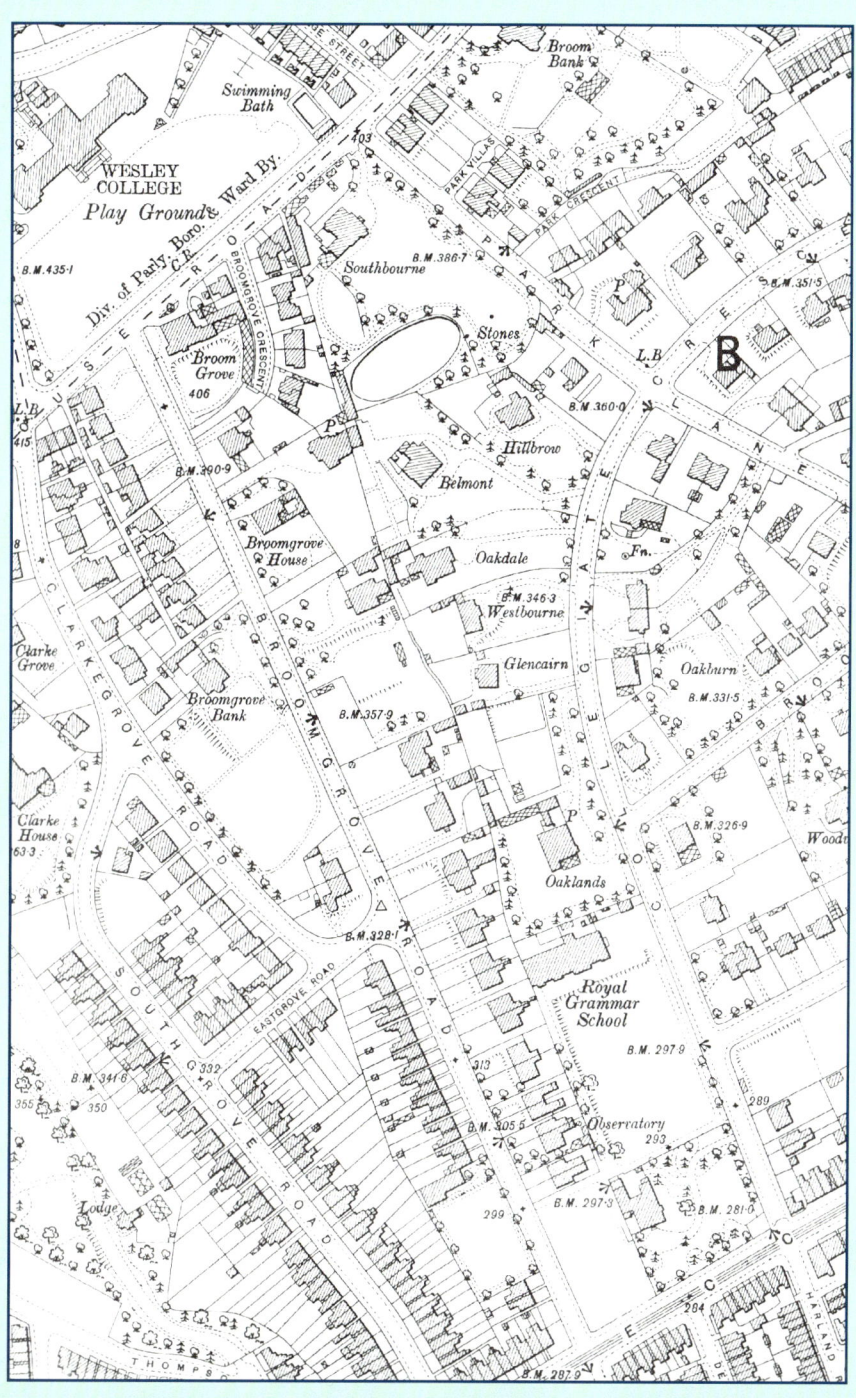

World War One

In 1914, seven colleges (Leeds, Sheffield, Brighton, Manchester, Armstrong, Chelsea and Kennington) were requisitioned, affecting 1,476 teacher training places. The hostels at Birmingham, Sheffield and Leeds became hospitals. At Sheffield, all the College premises were requisitioned as part of the 3rd Northern Base Hospital (which included Longshaw Lodge and Greystones School). The regimental headquarters of 212 (Yorkshire) Field Hospital were at Endcliffe Hall, under the command of Lt Col J Sinclair White, with eight officers and 167 other ranks. The hospital at Collegiate provided 400 beds, through which passed an incredible total of 64,555 sick and wounded men. The wounded British and Belgians began to arrive in August 1914 after the Battle of Mons.

King George V visiting the wounded in No.1 Tent behind Collegiate Hall

Christmas card showing Collegiate Hall in the background

Establishing the hospital caused severe damage to the College furnishings which had so recently been completed. The cubicle partitions were ripped out. On the lawns there were temporary huts used for recreation and prayer, and an operating theatre. Open-topped trolley buses and ambulances arrived full of wounded men, lean-to awnings along the lawns sheltered the beds of convalescing men from the sun, Christmas decorations adorned the wards and King George V came to visit. A Christmas card with the mascot - a crow - and a soldier on duty outside Collegiate Hall was printed. The College Principal, The Reverend Pearson, was chaplain to the wounded.

Lady Superintendent Mrs Henry may have stayed in her lodgings at Collegiate Hall as she commented on the strangeness of meeting *'men in khaki'* rather than *'girls in white blouses'*.

Teaching accommodation for the College moved back to the Wesleyan school rooms in Carver Street (used during building work when the College first opened), and apparatus and books were taken there so that work could resume in September 1914. A Junior described his first days in the Crescent magazine (1915), *'Next morning we set off for Carver Street with*

Celebrating Christmas in a hospital ward in Collegiate Hall

elaborate instructions… we found the building and hung round, too nervous to enter. Seeing another suspicious person loitering about, we… hazarded a simultaneous query 'Coll. Chap?' which was satisfactorily answered and we all three entered the building. We went into prayers three strong, and found we were greatly in the minority, for there were seventy-eight ladies!'… He sat an entrance exam a couple of weeks later, and the same night was invited to a 'Welcome Smoker'. 'Let us hope that next year… we shall be at Southbourne to welcome other students… to keep up Coll. traditions and pass them on to those that come after us.'

Bus carrying wounded soldiers turning into Collegiate Crescent

The male students had to make a decision between enlisting and continuing their training. A guarantee was made in January 1915 that all students who had completed one year of training would be given temporary recognition as a certificated teacher for two years, to be confirmed permanently if the LEA judged their teaching satisfactory. This led to a rush of volunteers and reduced student numbers in 1916 to 142 students.

In 1916 Sheffield University offered teaching accommodation and the College students moved out of the Carver Street rooms to use rooms at Western Bank - *'the 'swimming baths' of Carver Street have given place to the lecture rooms of the 'Varsity, and instead of crossing a graveyard, we now cross the quad…'*

Leather slippers found under the floor of Main Building during refurbishment in 2004-5

(Crescent 1916). The Seniors in 1916 were given their results and details of their teaching practice schools in Firth Hall, and the Vice Chancellor welcomed them - *'the teaching profession, he said, was a noble one. To be successful it was necessary that every teacher … should love her work,… and that she should enjoy good health. A good teacher filled the room with vitality'* (Crescent 1916).

Memorial plaque to World War One dead, now in Collegiate Learning Centre

Collegiate Campus buildings, 1905

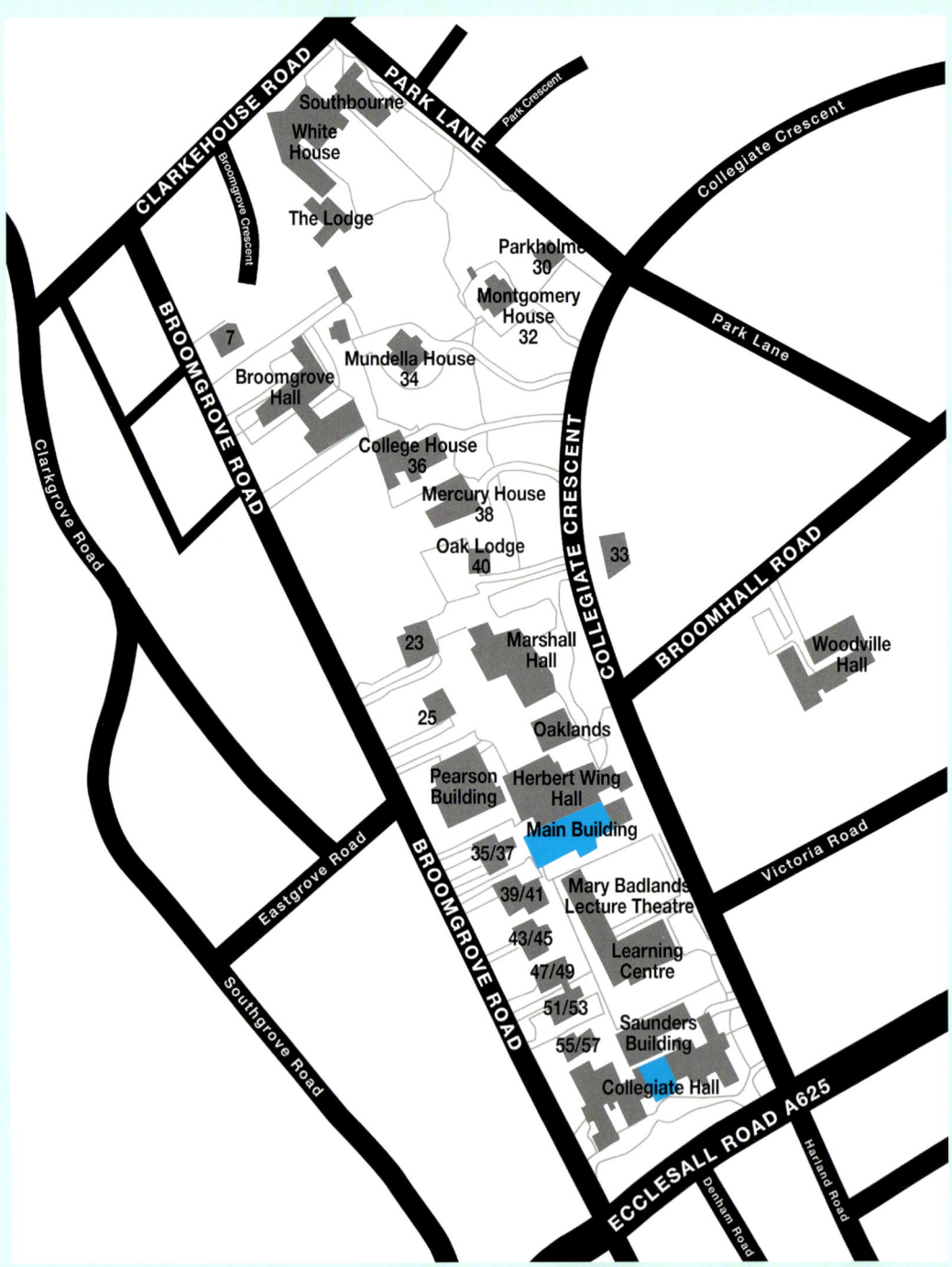

Collegiate Campus buildings, 1911

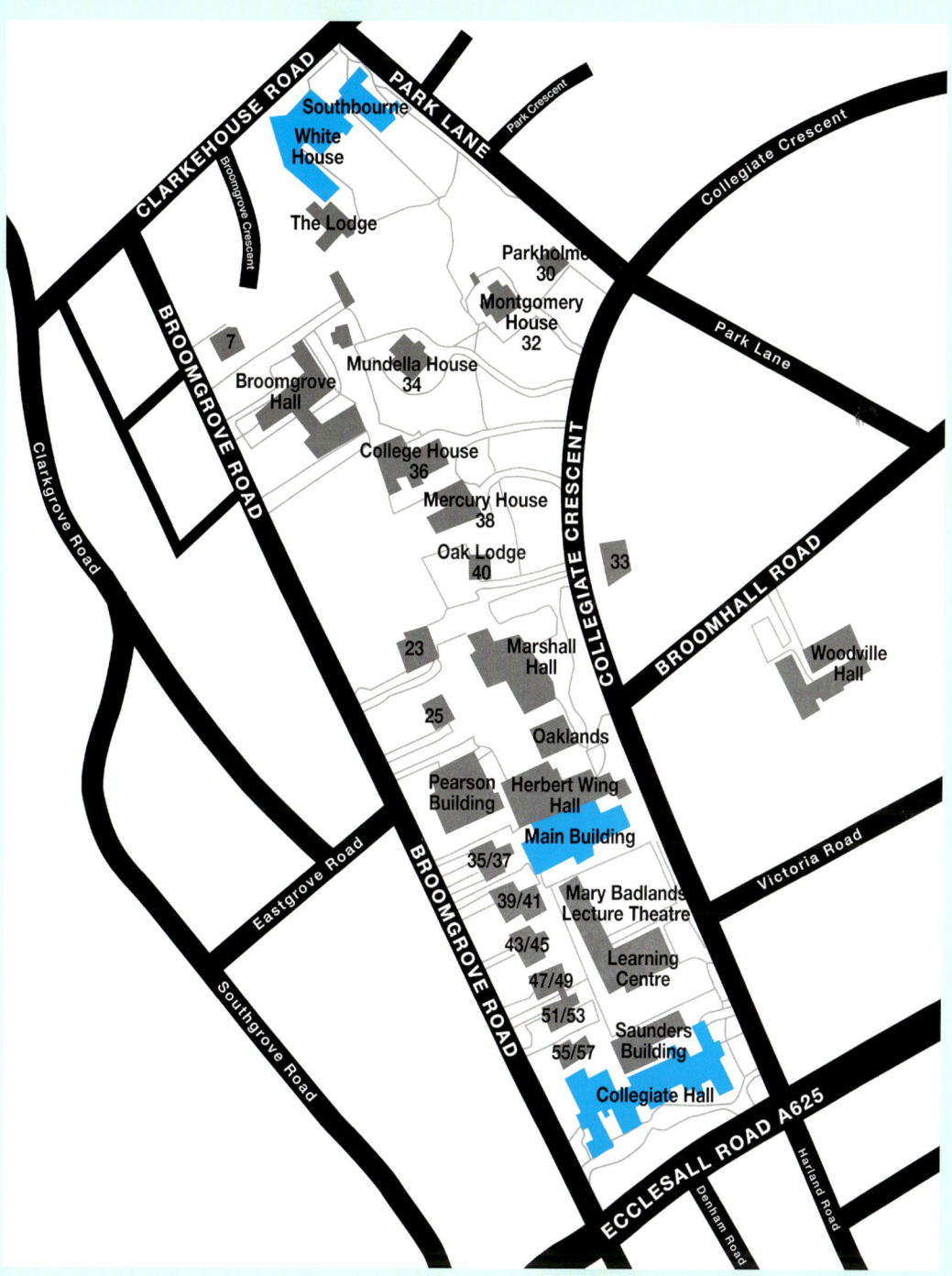

Sport

The College has developed a good reputation for physical education training, though not without setbacks. In the early 1920s it was briefly a leading national centre. During the mergers of the 1970s, Lady Mabel College at Wentworth Woodhouse, founded as a women's physical education college, joined the Polytechnic. Sheffield Hallam University maintains a strong commitment to sports science research and PE teacher training.

In the early days there was fierce competition in all sports both between houses of the College and with other regional colleges. At reunions there were 'past and present' student tournaments. Crescent (1954) reported on hostel sports, *'the inter-hostel football cup was won by the Daydreamers, who defeated Bottomgrove Bulls in the final. The No 11 (Broomgrove) Confederates knocked out the Park Penguins... the No.9 Butchers' Boys had their only victory against Topgrove United.'*

Gymkhana during World War One

In Collegiate Hall, cups awarded for sporting competitions resided on pedestals on either side of the dining hall - *'trophies are apt to wander, officially and unofficially, from the west side to the east side of the dining hall'*, and also between Juniors and Seniors. *'We (in West) are going to do our utmost to capture at least one more cup before the end of term so that East need not borrow our pedestals for their awards!'* (Crescent 1938).

The ground between Main Building and Collegiate Hall was fondly known as the *'cabbage patch'*, and was used as hockey pitches. In 1920 plans were drawn up for a physical training pavilion in the south-west corner of the open space behind 55-57 Broomgrove Road, but it was never built. Gym initially was taught in the hall of Main Building until a new one was built behind it in 1938, in which a climbing wall was installed in the 1970s. It was planned to build sports facilities at Lynwood (now Aunt Sally's) but the Pearson Sports Hall was ultimately built on Broomgrove Road in 1972, and remains a key social facility on the campus. There are also squash courts built by United Steels (now Corus) when they owned 32 and 34 Collegiate Crescent as graduate training venues, and all-weather football pitches and tennis courts near Southbourne, in an area which was once a lake.

Sport's Day, 1930

The first sports day was held in June 1906 and regularly thereafter.

In 1907 the HMI stressed the need for larger playing fields near the College, but none could be located; instead ten acres of land were bought on Derbyshire Lane in Norton in 1910 and a new pavilion was built. This was some distance from the College, and was also used by schools, College use being restricted to three afternoons a week. Students had to pay their tram fare to get there. Six tennis courts and a new pavilion were built in 1963 and the sports field has only recently ceased to be used.

Main Building Gym, 1944

Pearson Sports Hall, 1976

Pearson Sports Hall today

Sport

Hockey team, 1908

Swimming team, 1939

Football team, 1932-1933

Basketball team, 1952

Garden parties

Every summer the College held a Garden Party to raise funds for Dr Barnardo's, which in 1951 attracted about 1,000 people and raised over £200.

There were side shows, sales of work and tea, sports events and concerts. Before 1933 it was mainly organised by the female students at Collegiate Hall, but then began on a grander scale to involve all staff and students on the lawns at Southbourne and included an evening concert.

The 1946 programme was handwritten and included folk dancing, gymnastics display, extracts from plays, concert and dance, stalls and games, and an art and craft exhibition in the hostel common room. *'Many parents accompanied their sons to the hostel for a visit inspection and the rooms were viewed. The latter… were miraculously neat and tidy'* (Crescent 1946). Another undated programme had a similar range of events but charged a small admission to each; tea was 1/- (now 5p).

Programme from 1948

In 1950 the buildings were opened for view and students available to answer questions. Side shows included 'Av-a-go', golf and Punch and Judy, and 'bring and buy' stalls. Admission to the science exhibition was 6d - this included demonstrations of glass blowing, cellulose reactions, perspex and bakelite, and chemical experiments such as synthesis of insecticide!

Programme from 1950

World War Two

When war was declared in 1939, it was planned to evacuate the College to Loughborough along with Leeds students, but this never came about; *'in spite of visions of ourselves gliding along on our new bicycles at Loughborough, we were pleased to start the year in Collegiate Hall as usual, although black-out restrictions… had somewhat changed the aspect of the hostel'*. The men came to college until they reached military age and then could be awarded a certificate after five terms' attendance.

The College opened 11 weeks late while air-raid shelters were being built between Collegiate Hall and Ecclesall Road (which are still there), with *'a new task of blacking-out'*. While waiting to return to college, some students taught groups of children as part of a 'home-service' scheme. Oaklands was no longer a hostel, and the School Practice Library was turned into a Reading Room. Collegiate Hall lounge had acquired an electric radiator and new wireless set, and Miss Bowker sometimes invited the men students down (Crescent 1940). A barrage balloon named Ethel floated above the College grounds.

On 12-13 December 1940, during the night of the Sheffield Blitz, the upper floors in the old house in the centre of Collegiate Hall were occupied by 10 men taking turns on duty as firewatchers. Some women not in the shelters remained under the staircase of the old house. Bombs fell on the shops on Ecclesall Road opposite, and one student, Harry Daniels, was killed by the collapse of a tea merchants' shop as he helped to fight the fires. Collegiate Hall was made uninhabitable by bombing - windows and plaster were gone, slates came off the roof, and students rallied round to prepare tinned food, clear the debris and board the windows, before they returned to their homes. There are a number of holes and dents in the Collegiate Hall wall along Ecclesall Road which are reputed to have been caused by shrapnel during the blitz

Students in Southbourne were busy fire-watching, or refusing to shelter in order *'to see the fun!'* They came to help put fires out on the lawns of Southbourne and King Edward VII School, and to put out a fire caused by an incendiary on Park Lane. One student was injured by falling roof timbers.

Shrapnel hole in Collegiate Hall boundary wall on Ecclesall Road following a bomb blast opposite

One former student writes of Collegiate Hall, *'for the first year the boys fire-watched for us, but in the second year we had to take over. It involved two hourly shifts through the night, and a walk with a tiny torch light along the ground floor corridor to the opposite wing and we were more afraid of the many cockroaches than the bombs!'*

The College was open again by February 1941, and was able to carry on by economising with rationing allowances. Social events also continued, but the Crescent magazine ceased for four years due to shortage of paper. However the Principal's wife, Mrs

'Prinny' Kimbell, stepped in to write letters to students in the forces and put their photos on the music room wall as a 'Rogues Gallery', and Mr Kimbell created booklets from their news which were circulated. A copy of one of these newsletters survives, dated February 1944, sent to the Middle East; Kimbell received 160 replies to 500 letters sent out. He welcomed visits from men on leave, and noted that the 47 men and 124 women currently in College were very young (17-19). He gave an update on staff, and also listed the students who have been killed in action; 34 current and former students lost their lives and were commemorated with a plaque now in the Collegiate Learning Centre.

Memorial plaque to World War Two dead, now in Collegiate Learning Centre

Following the war, the College became an emergency training college, offering intensive training to demobilised men and women (a scheme which operated between 1945 and 1951). The returning mature students changed its character. The desperate need for accommodation led to emergency meetings in mid 1945 and the acquisition of Woodville (the old house being used as a YMCA hostel) at 21 Broomhall Road, 9 and 11 Broomgrove Road (old houses occupied by the Auxiliary Territorial Service), and Lynwood on Clarkehouse Road.

Accommodation

When the College opened in 1905, the first 27 female students were housed in the Lady Superintendent's house in the middle of Collegiate Hall until two wings were added to the house in 1906 and 1911, designed by architects Gibbs & Flockton. The building was innovative, as colleges at that time did not provide much residential accommodation. The press declared when the £10,000 west wing opened, *'there is no college in the kingdom so well arranged and fitted up'*.

Until the advent of mixed halls in the 1970s, women were housed at the lower end of the site, in Collegiate Hall, and later also in Fairfield (1 Broomhall Road) and Woodville. Men resided at the top end in Southbourne and Broomgrove.

Former school head's house at Collegiate Hall, first used for accommodation

In the Collegiate east (68 beds) and west (82 beds) wings, each girl had a 7x10 feet 'Irish boarded' cubicle containing a bed behind the door, wardrobe, dressing table, chair and wash table, and vent radiator. As there was ample study space, desks were not needed. *'In those Spartan days, cubicles were furnished with jugs and basins, water bottles and glasses. Students poised these on top of the corner cupboards…'* Some complained of *'cubicles in which there was no room to open wardrobe doors fully… the wooden chairs hard and calculated to wage victorious war on stockings…'* Two lady tutors lived in study bedrooms on each wing.

Dr Wing noted in 1962, *'It has always surprised me how much the students at Collegiate Hall were attached to their inconvenient building'*; *'this extraordinary and most inconvenient building has nevertheless had a warm place in the affections of many generations of women students.'*

In 1910 the old house at Southbourne was extended with two wings to house 60 men in shared rooms.

Those who could not live in College found lodging in the area. A 1910-12 student recalled, *'a family friend met us at the station and hired a taxi to take us to our lodgings at Wadborough Road. That was my first taxi ride and I think the fare was sixpence. We were in lodgings for two terms… we each paid our landlady fourteen shillings…'*

Early view of Collegiate Hall

Study at Collegiate Hall

Cubicle at Collegiate Hall

Collegiate Hall today

Sitting room at Collegiate Hall

Accommodation

The Crescent magazine (1915) carried some advice for landladies

- Don't expect punctuality at meals as students are very busy people.
- Don't forget *'Man shall not live by bread alone'*. Give him potted meat.
- Don't forget that Sheffield gas is cheap. Very few students have pink eyes.
- If soap is expensive don't fail to put the student in a damp bed. It might save washing in the morning.

During World War One, when the College was being used as a hospital, Ranmoor College on Fulwood Road housed 16 students; it had been a Methodist New Connexion college founded in 1860 by Thomas Firth and closed in 1917. It was bought in 1920 for £11,000 and used briefly to house the men students doing new PE courses. The College also rented 60/62 Clarkehouse Road for 28 students in 1917.

Bedroom at Southbourne

Southbourne today

The College continued with little change until student numbers increased in 1930 and Oaklands was acquired to accommodate 30 men. Following World War Two and growth through emergency training, 9 and 11 Broomgrove Road (old houses on the site of the present hall), were bought to house 36 men, with two flats for married tutors, and the original Woodville house (for 14 women) and Fairfield on Broomhall Road (for 18 women) were purchased, paving the way for later development. Many of the old houses on Broomgrove Road were used as residences at different times.

Parkholme at 30 Collegiate Crescent (for 17 men) and Hallam Lodge in Crosspool (28 men) opened in 1959; as Parkholme was not ready in September, a makeshift dormitory was arranged in the Southbourne games room for *'blithe spirits… amid a welter of table-tennis balls'*.

Fairfield on Broomhall Road

Student lino-cut of Fairfield

Oaklands in the 1960s

Accommodation

By the end of the 1950s, student numbers were increasing rapidly and urgent action was needed. By 1962 Marshall, Broomgrove and Woodville Halls had been built, the last two by demolishing Victorian houses, to provide a further 400 bed spaces, and allowed Collegiate Hall to be turned into teaching accommodation. The halls are of *'reinforced concrete grid-like frames with brick infill'* (Harman & Minnis 2004), designed by local architects Hadfield, Cawkwell & Davidson. Marshall cost £136,000 to build.

There were logistical challenges to keeping the College running at this time; men students in particular recall being moved from hall to hall almost each term, as the staff protected the sensitivities of the women. *'Buildings rising over grey gables… Sheffield will surely be proud to claim one of the finest colleges in the country'* (Crescent 1960).

Principal Herbert Wing said he *'prefers (*Marshall*) (to those in other colleges) for... architectural interest and furnishings'*. Features were cork floors, mahogany desks, pin-up boards and a kitchen-utility room on each floor. An 'old student' on seeing the new residences commented - *'they ought to have preserved just one of the old prison cells as a museum piece!'* (Prospectus 1968).

Broomgrove Hall of Residence

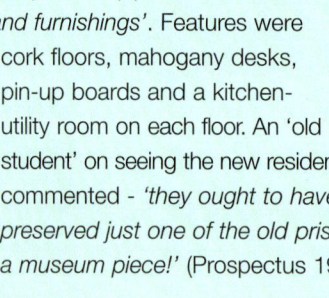

Tiles in the entrance porch to Broomgrove Hall

Marshall Hall of Residence

In 1968 single and shared study bedrooms were available for 649 students (about half the total), with women in Southbourne, Marshall, Woodville, Fairfield and Hallam Lodge, and men in Broomgrove hall and houses, and Lynwood. The last, now Aunt Sally's pub, had been acquired in about 1960 and almost became part of the campus when it was planned to build major new sports facilities there; these were subsequently built on Broomgrove Road.

Woodville Hall of Residence

By 1975 many more buildings had been acquired or built, and mixed accommodation had been increased to a total of 1626 beds, of which 1044 beds were residential, in Ballard, Broomgrove, Mundella (for the fourth year BEds), Marshall, Southbourne, Woodville, and the halls acquired with the merger of Totley College - Highfield and Lowfield, and 582 beds were self-catering in small houses and in a new student village in Norfolk Park. Woodville Lodge (in front of Woodville) was the day students' hostel.

Crescent magazine cover from 1960

Accommodation

Southbourne ceased to be residential accommodation in 1988. Highfield and Lowfield have been demolished and Ballard is awaiting redevelopment. However, the three 1960s halls continue to provide over 400 catered rooms on campus.

1960s bedroom

Cartoon from the Crescent magazine, 1963

Lynwood, now Aunt Sally's Pub

Growth and merger

Much of the College's turbulent history in the 1960s and 1970s was related to national demographics. But national planning for Education provision scarcely made for clarity or well managed change. The outlines of the growth in student numbers are straightforward. By 1960 the College had 426 enrolled trainees, having catered for 189 students in 1910. Numbers had thus doubled in 50 years, with the major increase being immediately after World War Two, from 276 in 1945 to 348 in 1947, followed by a spurt in the late 1950s, from 367 in 1957-1958 to 426 two years later. The shifts of the mid 1940s resulted from pent-up demand during wartime and the decision made by national government in 1944 to raise the school leaving age. The substantial growth of the late 1950s reflected the impact on school enrolments of the post-1945 baby boom and an increase of 43 per cent between 1956 and 1961 in the proportion of 16-18 year olds taking A levels.

While the growth of the late 1950s was substantial in historical terms, it was trivial by the standards of what happened in the 1960s. The number of trainees trebled from 426 in 1959-1960 to 1310 in 1969-1970. This rise reflected the impact upon the national demand for teachers of the new baby boom of the late 1950s and early 1960s, the rise in the average school leaving age, and the vast surge in the proportion of 18-year olds who took A levels, from nine per cent in 1961 to one-third ten years later. It also reflected the shift from two-year to three-year training courses. Moreover, in the early 1960s about 30 per cent of newly qualified women teachers left the profession before reaching the age of 30.

The 1960s produced an explosive boom in teacher education accompanied by the transformation of the training colleges into colleges of education and a general growth in their size. Sheffield's own trebling of trainee numbers matched the increase in the teacher training sector as a whole. By the end of the 1960s, the colleges of education had more students than the universities had held a decade earlier and, in terms of student numbers, were the second largest grouping of institutions providing post-18 education (see table on page 40). British universities enrolled 225,000 students in 1968, while the colleges enrolled 126,000. The new Sheffield City College of Education was substantially smaller than the University of Sheffield, but it provided far more full-time post-18 education than did the College of Technology and Arts. It was among the largest dozen or so of the 157 colleges of education. The boom had been accompanied also by a large programme of building and property acquisition. At the end of the decade Herbert Wing's dream of expanding the campus to fill the Collegiate site from Clarkehouse Road to Ecclesall Road had been to a large extent fulfilled.

At the moment of their greatest institutional success the colleges of education faced their greatest planning challenge. By the late 1960s it was clear that there would be very limited growth in the demand for teachers during the 1970s and into the 1980s. The only way in which teacher trainee numbers would expand significantly was through a large reduction in class sizes. By 1973 and an increasingly dire financial outlook for the national budget, that prospect was gloomier than even pessimists of the late 1960s would have predicted. In national planning, the demand for university places was seen as surging in the 1970s, and what was then called the Further Education sector, embracing the colleges of technology and art and the polytechnics created from 1969, was planned to more than double in size. From being the second sector to the universities, the colleges were to be overtaken by the Further Education sector from the mid-1970s and left very far behind by the early 1980s.

Growth in teacher training providers in England and Wales

Year	Approximate number of providers	Types of provider	Total number of trainees
1850	16		991
1858	35		2,965
1870	34		2,495 (26% of children attending school)
1890	49	6 Day Training Colleges in universities	3,679 (57% of children attending school)
1902	63	45 residential 17 Day Training Colleges 1 college for blind	5,800 (output 2,800 teachers annually)
1905	72		8,987
1914	89	47 voluntary 22 LEA colleges	13,356
1916	72		9,033
1920	92		15,451
1929	108	20 University Training Depts 77 2 year colleges 11 domestic subject colleges	
1937	109	22 University Training Depts 75 2 year colleges 11 domestic subject colleges	15,236
1939		63 voluntary 28 LEA colleges	
1944	100	62 2 year colleges 22 University Training Depts 11 domestic subject colleges 6 PE colleges	15,000
1947		55 new emergency training colleges	
1951	132	56 voluntary 76 LEA colleges	25,000
1958	140	98 with less than 200 students, 3 with 500+	30,000

1962	146	48 voluntary 98 LEA colleges	50,000
1970	157		120,000
1971	160		114,000
1976	110 down to 39	c12 colleges to close 25% each to be free-standing, merge with Polytechnics, merge with FE colleges or merge with other colleges	35,000

Degree day, 1976

The colleges entered the debate of the early 1970s over their future role from a difficult position. The Robbins Report of 1963 had argued for the independence of the colleges - separating them from local authority control - and the alignment of the colleges for what we would nowadays call quality assurance and enhancement functions with the universities. These recommendations had eventually been rejected by Harold Wilson's Labour government, at least partly on the ground that the Department of Education needed to keep full responsibility for planning and funding trainee numbers, and shaping the character and content of professional preparation. The Labour government also pushed the creation of 30 polytechnics from 1969, with an original target of 2,000 full-time higher education students each (in addition to their extensive part-time and 16-18 year old provision). By 1970-1971 many experts saw the new polytechnics as likely to move fairly quickly to 5,000 such higher education students each if the projected explosion in qualified students materialised.

When planned student numbers on this scale were bandied about, the 157 colleges of education of 1970 began to look distinctly small. Although they had expanded considerably in the 1960s, only 22 of them had over 1,000 students, and they had no chance, as monotechnics, of keeping pace with the universities or, more significantly, the new, consolidated polytechnics. Sheffield City College was one of the country's largest, but was still constrained by the national constriction on further growth. One possibility was amalgamation of education colleges in the sub-region. Sheffield and the near region contained three colleges formed to cope with the demand for additional teacher training after 1945. Thornbridge in north Derbyshire was for women only and had 250 students in 1970. Totley, with 750 students, specialised in Home Economics and Primary. Lady Mabel College, originally established after World War Two as a physical education college and still specialising in that subject, had 380 women students at a spectacular, leased country house at Wentworth Woodhouse, under the Rotherham local authority. Thornbridge and Totley, sharing a concentration on Primary, merged in 1971. But exploratory discussions from Sheffield City College about merger led nowhere.

The dilemma facing Harry Peake, the Principal, was an acute one. Dr. Peake had succeeded Herbert Wing in 1965. Peake had an Oxford First, had used his mathematics and physics in wartime work at Bletchley, and had been a headmaster of a grammar school. A committed Christian, he was a strong and persuasive personality who often had a powerful influence upon individuals' future careers with his advice and sense of values and direction. He was also a national figure in the education college sector, serving as chairman of the ATCDE (the Association of Teachers in College and Departments of Education) in 1972-1973. He was extremely well placed to understand and shape national and, in his mind also, local policy. The dilemmas he and the College faced were academic, institutional, and political.

On the academic front, Peake and the College set great store by their entry standards and reputation for providing a rigorous programme of study. The College had plenty of applicants for trainee places, and was in the higher range of colleges (certainly in the region) in terms of A level entry requirements. In 1969, 64 per cent of its entrants had two or more A levels, which were required as the threshold for university entrance. Some 70 per cent of women entrants made that threshold in contrast to only 46 per cent of men; but men constituted under a quarter of the total entry. To reinforce this claim to academic strength and following Wing's lead from the late 1940s, appointments to lecturing posts were made on the basis of sound academic aptitude. Some academic departments had established good reputations. At the same time, College staff had worked hard with the University of Sheffield's Institute of

Education (a semi-autonomous body responsible for validating teacher education awards among a number of partner colleges) to gain academic credibility. Education as a degree subject was only just emerging in the late 1960s, with the first BEd degrees being awarded in 1968, validated nationwide by only five universities. The University of Sheffield was among that first cluster and Sheffield City College was thus a pioneer in running a BEd. By 1972 some 23 universities were awarding the degree. But the majority of successful candidates nationally in the years 1970-1972 secured pass degrees or Thirds. There was still a long way to go in order to achieve parity of Education degree programmes compared with other university degree subjects.

Good entry qualifications and an effective relationship with the University of Sheffield's Institute of Education led Peake in a direction to which his own background and inclinations impelled him anyway. But at a time, in the early 1970s, when many academic planners were urging greater flexibility in programme development, more interdisciplinarity, and more adventurous curriculum experimentation, the insistence on the centrality of academic disciplines in a general sense and as a key element in thinking about future provision struck a discordant note. The stress on academic values was perfectly understandable in the context of the struggle, still proceeding, to gain recognition for Education as an acceptable subject. But it sounded increasingly defensive and traditional.

In considering Sheffield City College's institutional position, Peake naturally based his thinking on the relative strength of the College in providing higher education. In terms of full-time degree and diploma students, the College of Education had been larger than the city's College of Technology and Arts, which became part of the new Polytechnic. To underscore this strength - shared by the colleges of education as a sector - Peake made two points which became difficult to maintain in terms of higher education planning in the 1970s. One argument in such planning was that there would be an increasing student demand for a whole range of vocational courses and part-time routes, some of which would necessarily be at the non-degree level. Peake made plain his distaste for the large-scale development of sub-degree and other courses, *'the change in role and ethos could be a traumatic experience. The staff of a typical college of education has not ventured into the Further Education jungle...'* This language closed down rather than opened up opportunities. His second emphasis developed from the relationship with the University of Sheffield. He pressed the desirability of university validation of Education programmes. This was vital, in his view, because the universities enjoyed *'relative freedom from national and local political pressures'*, in contrast, potentially, to the CNAA. In addition, he argued that, *'teachers will never achieve professional status if their employer has a dominant influence within the validating agency'*. The very agency which polytechnics saw as their vehicle for academic development and diversification was implicitly contrasted unfavourably with the full professional status which only university validation could ensure. These two points together made it difficult for Sheffield City College to become the city's third higher education institution. On the one hand, the option of diversifying from monotechnic specialism was narrowed by the scepticism shown towards non-degree work. On the other hand, the very status of the profession was described as reliant upon independent university validation.

At the national level, the ATCDE, of which Peake later became chairman, argued in 1970 that the college sector could double in size. Some education planning experts conceded that there might be a case of expansion, *'if the colleges develop into major centres of social work training or, some of them, into liberal arts colleges'*. But critics noted of the ATCDE proposals that they were not clear on cognate disciplines or fully informed of new developments. It was also stressed that enthusiasm for diversification had come late to the ATCDE, which in 1969 had reiterated its identification with teacher training. By the early and mid 1970s it was becoming clear nationally that expansion in vocationally focused courses such as social work and growing student demand for social sciences and humanities programmes were being met within the new polytechnics and that some flexible and innovative interdisciplinary and cross-disciplinary options were being provided for students.

The third dilemma challenging the College and its Principal was political. It was obvious by the late 1960s that the demand for HE would expand massively in the 1970s. Full-time HE numbers in Britain had more that doubled between 1959-1960 and 1968-1969, from 170,000 to 443,000. Projections from the late 1960s suggested that the total would almost double again to 847,000 by 1981-1982. The actual numbers involved far exceeded the increase occurring in the 1960s. Financial calculation meant eventually that the universities would not get a large share of that growth. And the collapse of anticipated teacher numbers, together with the adaptiveness of the polytechnics, meant that the colleges of education did not become the vehicles for expansion. The polytechnics' responsiveness made them friends across the political spectrum. To many Labour politicians, they represented an important move away from elitist institutions and towards HE opening widely to local communities and new approaches to teaching, learning and flexible progression. In Sheffield a new generation of Labour politicians involved in city government - David Blunkett most notably was first elected in 1970 when Labour took 63 seats to the Conservatives' 44 and Liberals' 1 - identified the Polytechnic as the local institutional route to social and educational transformation. Somewhat paradoxically, many businessmen saw the polytechnics as more responsive to business and industrial needs and to the skills agenda than were the more remote, traditional universities. Margaret Thatcher, as Secretary of State for Education in 1970-1974, almost preferred the more applied programmes offered by polytechnics to the more theoretical approach followed in much traditional university work and she took up her department's advocacy of the new Diploma of Higher Education as a means of widening access. Fostered under Labour, the polytechnics became the lead partners in mergers with colleges of education under the Conservatives in 1973. The decision for Sheffield was made public in the autumn of that year. Nothing could have been further removed from the Robbins' recommendation for incorporating teacher training into the universities delivered only ten years earlier.

Despite the recommendation of the local education authority and the line of preference within the Department of Education in London, Dr. Peake waged a campaign, publicly noted in January 1974, to secure the college's future as a separate college of higher education, possibly strengthened by merging with Totley-Thornbridge.

The problem with this proposal was that the size of an officially acceptable institution was expanding rapidly in the 1970s. Although planners in the Department of Education and Science conceded that there might be generalist higher education institutions with only 1,000-2,000 students if they concentrated on the social sciences and arts, they were also pressing for the expansion of the polytechnics. Existing degree-level work in the colleges would boost that aspect of the polytechnics' portfolios and the predominantly female student populations of the colleges would produce a more even gender mix in the merged institutions. All this was compounded by the realisation that the birth-rate was falling very rapidly in the early 1970s, far more rapidly than the planners had foreseen. The national demand for trained teachers was about to plunge. Setting up a third higher education institution in Sheffield and similarly placed cities did not make strategic sense. Moreover, the local education authorities were responsible for the polytechnics and two-thirds of the education colleges, and they uniformly chose to merge them if they funded one of each. Those colleges which survived and diversified were in towns where there was no polytechnic -

Edge Hill in Ormskirk has, notably, since become a large higher education institution - or were church colleges, such as Canterbury Christ Church, Chester, St. Martin's in Lancaster or York St. John's.

Any alternative strategy of joining or partnering the University of Sheffield would have been an unusual one in the circumstances of the early 1970s. The universities as a whole had no interest in expanding social science and humanities degree work, under their validation, within the colleges of education. Worse, the government's planning White Paper of 1972 indicated that any incorporation of the colleges into the universities would have to be covered from the individual universities' existing allocation of funded student numbers. That plainly indicated Whitehall's preferred outcome.

As soon as the outline decision for merger, also involving Totley-Thornbridge, was announced in late 1973, it was clear that the government's and local education committee's thinking required a thorough reorganisation of the new institution. One possibility was to consolidate teacher training in one college (presumably Collegiate) while using the other (presumably Totley-Thornbridge) for the new two-year Dip.HE. But that would not have met the expectation of flexibility and the belief, as the *Morning Telegraph* put it, that *'teachers should no longer live and learn in isolation but mix with other students and other disciplines'*. Given that the total number of trainees fell to 800 by 1981 - not only for City College and Totley-Thornbridge but also for Lady Mabel College - the numerical significance of Education within the vastly expanded Polytechnic shrank substantially. That reduction was accompanied by academic dispersal.

Institutional cultures are difficult to define but are often critically important. The merger of 1976 raised major issues of institutional attitudes and customs for many of the staff involved. It would be quite wrong to suggest a simple contrast between an Education culture and the culture of the new Polytechnic. For many staff there were strong differences of attitude between Totley-Thornbridge (which was said to be more focussed on teaching practice) and City College (which claimed for itself more emphasis on academic subjects). But many involved in the merger felt that the Polytechnic's management style was more informal - some have used stronger words - and its academic approach less traditional than that of the College. Some academic managers have argued that the validation and revalidation procedures required by CNAA were beneficially rigorous and marked a considerable shift from the more relaxed approach to programme validation adopted by the universities. From a very modest involvement with BEd degrees in 1970, the CNAA was validating programmes which registered 38 per cent of all BEd students in 1982. Within the CNAA framework of validation many in the Polytechnic saw the 1970s as a golden age of programme innovation, opening up the exploration of new curricular opportunities freed from prevailing models of what should be taught in an 'acceptable' degree syllabus. Part of that ethos was that service teaching - with a subject offering modules across a number of degrees in different subjects - was common and positively fostered.

The biggest changes came in how Education was organised and how the students' status in relation to an institutional ethos was defined.

From the Polytechnic's perspective the challenge posed by merger was immense. The total number of trainees from the two colleges in 1976 was 1800. By 1981 that number had fallen to 800, the result of government action in response to the Department of Education's projections of the demand for teachers. Staff numbers greatly exceeded teaching needs, and early retirements, under financially generous national agreements, followed. But a major decision had to be made as to the location of academic subjects and, as in other polytechnics, the outcome was to disperse lecturers in 'academic' subjects to join existing, or form new, departments within the Polytechnic.

The pattern of teaching was to change dramatically. In the three-year course, developed by the late 1960s, students were required to engage with five different areas of study and practice. During those three years they spent about one-fifth of their time on teaching practice, with a concentration in the very last term of the third year. They spent about 80 per cent of their time, divided roughly equally, on each of Principles of Education, Professional Courses, and two main subjects. The level of attainment in those main subjects was up to pass degree level. Students seeking the BEd needed to complete an additional year studying two *'academic'* subjects to general degree level. When first introduced the BEd, was undertaken at the University of Sheffield, but was available at the College from 1969. As an indication of the underpinnings of the 'academic' subjects, the most frequently chosen main subjects in 1966-1967 were

	Number of students
English	160
Geography	133
History	114
French	95
Biology	65
Mathematics	61
Religious knowledge	54

Nine other subjects under 50 each

The staff teaching these academic subjects were widely dispersed within the Polytechnic. By the early 1980s, for instance, geography and environmental studies were at Wentworth Woodhouse, English and history were at Totley, mathematics and science were at Pond Street. Only the specialists within Education remained together, eventually forming part of a new Faculty of Education, Health and Welfare. A separate, small department of Education Management from the Polytechnic joined the Faculty. Within the Education department, there were separate groups in Education Studies and Professional Practice, maintaining an organisational differentiation which had long existed.

Naturally, there were disagreements over the re-organisation. But academic departments and the specialists in Education theory and practice had long operated separately within the College. In the late 1960s students taking the three-year course studied two academic disciplines throughout the programme and devoted about 40 per cent of their time to Education, which all students took together. They were out in schools for four weeks in year one, five weeks in year two, and for the whole of the third term in year three. Students in the 1970s felt that the academic subjects were, generally, well and thoroughly taught. But they were not necessarily taught in ways directly linked to pedagogic ideas and issues. By moving the academic sections into existing departments, the Polytechnic sought to strengthen the range and depth of its departmental offering. The growth of student numbers in the 1980s, directed away from the universities and towards the polytechnics, reinforced the logic of that move.

However, such a move directly reduced the size and influence of Education as a separate subject within the Polytechnic. Some staff saw this as a deliberate move to reduce the significance of the subject in the enlarged institution. Others were sceptical about the cohesion of an Education agenda, vision or voice and about the extent of research development among the College's subjects. A possible gain from merging subjects was the enhancement of an emerging research culture by joining the College's academic departments with those of the Polytechnic. Some of those involved have suggested that the tutors in academic subjects favoured merger and integration by subject discipline. For many academics the new subject departments worked very effectively and the Polytechnic in the 1980s fostered individuals' postgraduate work and research.

But this dramatic internal transformation has to be seen against two national trends. In 1972 some 50,632 new entrants - an all-time high - were admitted to Initial Teacher Training courses in England and Wales. In 1980 that number of new entrants had slumped to 19,149, the lowest for decades. A decline was always planned, but it got steadily worse in the early to mid 1970s as the birth rate, and therefore future demand for teachers, fell far more than predicted. In 1977 there were 569,000 live births. At the height of the baby boom of the late 1950s and early 1960s that number had reached 876,000 in 1964. There were fewer live births in 1977 than there had been in the worst year of the economic depression in 1933 or in the most threatening year of World War Two, in 1940, which were the previous trough years. To make matters worse, the national economy hit increasing difficulties from 1973 onwards, ensuring that no allowance could be made in the budget to reduce class sizes and thereby prop up some of the demand for new teachers. But if this was not bad enough, there was a purely internal development within teacher training which made the late 1970s and early 1980s even worse for former college providers. The grand total of new entrants fell dramatically from 1972. But within that total a major shift occurred. The number of one-year PGCE candidates admitted to training courses rose slightly. The government's objective of making teaching a graduate profession was being advanced by more graduates entering training rather than by more students taking the BEd route. In 1972 a massive 37,381 new entrants to Initial Teacher Training enrolled for the three or four-year routes. In 1980 only 7,017 did so. The national demand for the courses which accounted for nearly all the Colleges' student numbers had fallen by 80 per cent.

Changes within the College did not simply involve an adjustment to these numerical transformations. One aspect of the College's culture transformed by the merger was the relationship between student life and institutional regulations. When Herbert Wing arrived he tried to provide a more liberal approach to the College's regulation of students' lives which, by all accounts, was more strict than that of the universities in the 1950s. The difficulties were considerable. The first Principal had been a Methodist Minister and many felt that there was an ethos of non-conformist austerity about the city and the College. The College admitted males and females from its founding, still not a typical characteristic of training colleges into the 1950s, but had taught them separately until the 1930s. Many students resided in the College but day students, securing more freedom, also gained admission. Especially after World War Two, and during the continuation of national service, many men students were older and more accustomed to being away from home than most of the women students were. Yet attitudes from the 1930s continued to influence some members of staff. It seems likely that, on average, women students came from slightly more affluent backgrounds than male students, and family pressures upon women ran against seeking marriage with fellow trainees. Early marriage created enormous financial problems until the 1940s, since a married woman had to resign from a teaching post. For those women who went to, or were pushed into, training colleges as alternatives if they failed to gain admission to university and for those who treated the period of attendance almost as the equivalent of a finishing school, there was no reason to establish serious relationships with male trainees. When Wing proposed in the 1950s easing up on the weekend residential restrictions, he received protests from parents who expected their daughters to be kept under supervision while at College. At Thornbridge, a women's college, a visiting male NUS representative was carefully confined to one room during his visit. At Lady Mabel, even fathers were not allowed to visit their daughters' rooms. Such restrictions had begun to change in the 1960s. Peake ensured that a bar was opened in 1971, against the initial opposition of older staff. A mixed residential hall opened. Strong support encouraged more mature students to enrol. In 1968 some 26 students aged between 26 and 48 joined the first course specially aimed at mature students and all of them successfully completed it three years later. By 1970, students at City College residences were permitted to 'entertain visitors in their rooms' from 12.00pm to 22.45pm. But restrictions remained. Only by signing for an extension were students allowed not to be in the residential halls after 11.00pm. The Academic Board, strongly representing older heads of department, voted not to permit the students' drama group - which depended on staff support - to stage 'The Bald-headed Prima Donna', as being unsuitable for a student production. When the decision was made, at the end of a lengthy debate, one member announced *sotto voce* that anyone wishing to see the play could go to the forthcoming production at High Storrs School.

This degree of regulation became increasingly anachronistic in relation both to changing social mores and to the legal lowering of the age of adulthood from 21 to 18 years. Yet for many of the older staff in particular the College's official role *in loco parentis* and its mission to provide an all-embracing experience, through organised games, social events, music, drama and so forth, remained integral to the provision of teacher training. In terms of the College as a total institution the merger in 1976 firmly ended an era. Many College staff regretted the passing of what they viewed as a happy collegial existence often led with some style. Equally, many staff embraced the Polytechnic's emphasis upon providing education and support services to students without seeking to mould their lifestyles into a model based on selected aspects of middle-class activities or aspirations.

Collegiate Campus buildings, 1950

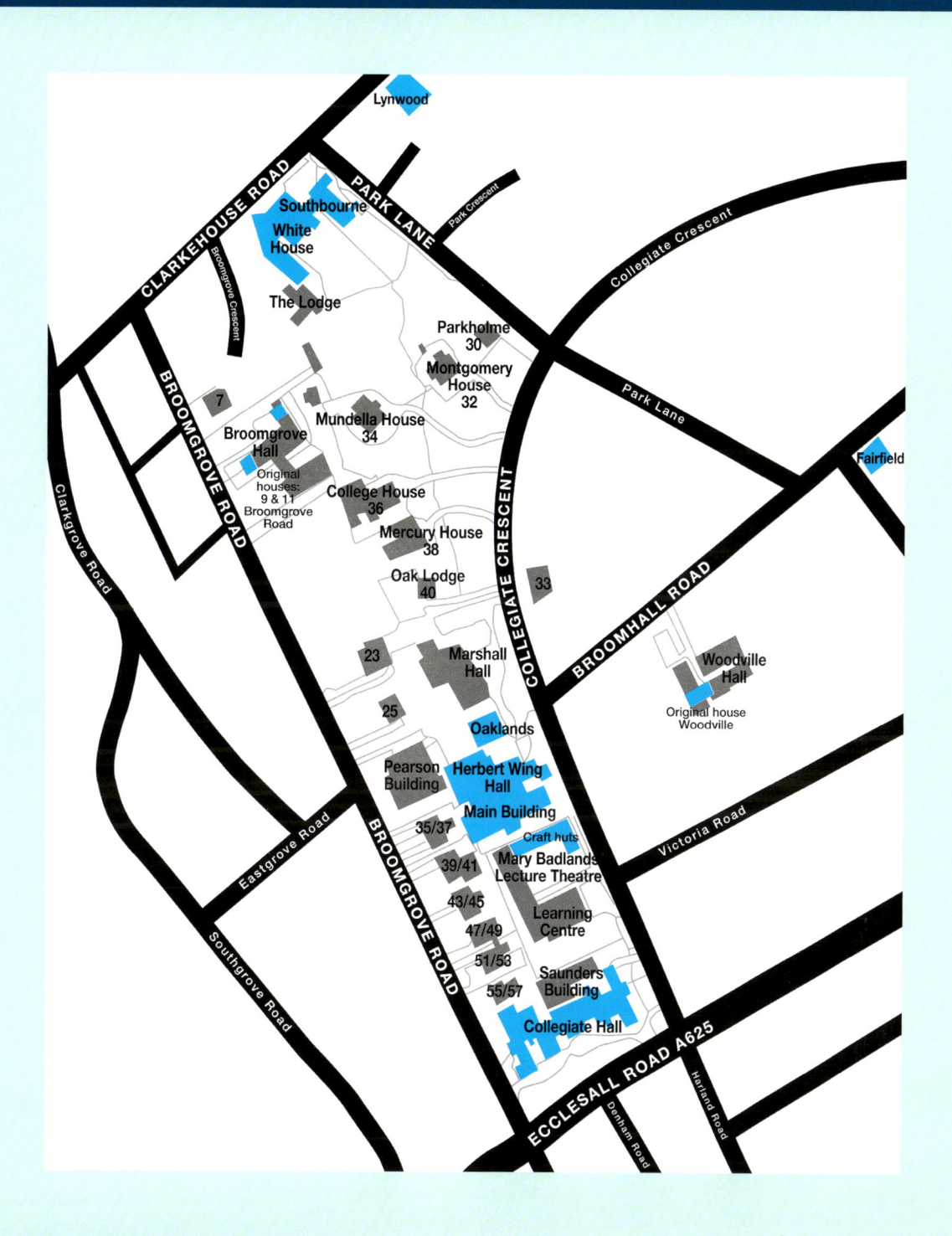

School practice

Prior to the 1902 Education Act, training colleges set up their own model, practice and demonstration schools to enable their students to put theory into practice. The Act placed all elementary schools under the new LEAs and one of their conditions of grant was the obligation to take practising students. The minimum length of practice started at six weeks over the two years, but was quickly increased to 12 weeks.

Sheffield City Training College and now Sheffield Hallam University have maintained close links throughout the century with the nearby Hunter's Bar, Pomona and Springfield Schools. Almost all practice took place within Sheffield boundaries in the early days; students in the mid 1940s recall being the first to be sent to Rotherham.

In the late 30s, women's dress for teaching practice included a white blouse, navy skirt, coat and hat, black stockings and shoes.

Crescenters Committee at the 2005 Reunion in the refurbished tiered lecture room, originally used for criticism lessons

The 1935 inspection report noted that most students arrived with one year's student teacher experience, and then improved their skills through Continuous Practice, Group Criticism Lessons (one taught while others observed), Technical Exercises (given by one while others observed) and Demonstration Lessons. School Practice occupied two weeks each in the 3rd, 4th and 5th terms, and one additional week in either the 2nd or 4th term. *'The College takes a very serious view of its responsibilities in regard to the students' professional training, and the time given to it is probably more than in most colleges.'*

Small groups of children from a neighbouring school came in for weekly classes with first year trainees, and were delighted with the arrangement. They were crocodiled into the tiered lecture room for criticism lessons. The dreaded *'crits'* were a traditional feature of training at all colleges; believed to be *'curative and formative'*, they actually caused students *'acute distress'* (Dent 1977) and were artificial.

In the late 1930s, there was an unwritten league table of schools, ranging from 'paradise' to 'undisciplined!'

By the time of the 1955 inspection, practice occupied four three-week blocks in autumn and spring terms of each year, and staff supervised 12-14 students each.

By 1960 more practice facilities were needed; it was felt that all schools should take their share, and it was recommended that a school practice committee should be set up to include teachers.

Women on school practice, wearing overalls, 1938

Wing (1965) considered that the problem of providing places for teaching practice was not recognised nationally; as a minimum, two out of three teachers should expect to have a trainee for three months of the year. He recommended that an experienced teacher should be in charge of trainees in a school. He paid tribute to the schools used for teaching practice. At that time one Principal Lecturer was responsible for placing 1,000 students.

In 1968 the three year route included 18 weeks of teaching practice: four weeks at the end of year one autumn term, five weeks at the end of year two spring term, and nine weeks in year three summer term. In 1975 students spent 60 days in school on the PGCE route.

Today trainees are required to spend 24 out of 36 weeks on the one year PGCE route on teaching practice, provided through partnerships with over 800 regional schools.

Timetable for school practice at Sharrow Lane School, 1930

Libraries

The first College libraries were study rooms in the halls of residence, in the east wings in both Collegiate Hall and Southbourne. By the 1930s, the library stocked some 4,000 books, and the Crescent magazine reported that the most popular general literature writers were Agatha Christie, Eric Linklater and Richard Aldington. The 1935 HMIs stated that *'the books are contained in bookcases with open shelves. These are set at right angles to the long walls so as to form bays which are useful for study, for which purpose there is an adequate supply of tables and chairs.'* The library budget was £48. It was recommended that the library be transferred to the Main Building but subject libraries were held within departments until the late 1940s.

Main Building library

The HMI inspection in 1955 reported on the library, by then housed in the central hall of Main Building, with *'well designed and dignified furniture, though an unfortunate effect is produced by the brickwork which shows above the bookcases'*. A member of the Education staff supervised the library, having catalogued and classified (on the Dewey system) the whole collection of 7,700 books when it was moved to one place in 1950. The collection was reported to be of suitable standard but lacking in works of scholarship. It had a grant of £300 to cover everything, from rebinding to the purchase of new books and periodicals. There was no acquisition policy. The school practice library was in Collegiate Hall, with 3,000 books and managed by a member of the English staff. The routine work was done by students, who all took a practical course on the organisation of school libraries.

In 1960 three adjoining libraries were established in the Main Building - the main library where it currently was, the school practice library in what had been the common room and the reference library in the chemistry lab. The library books were moved from Collegiate Hall to Main Building *'by a continuous column of volunteer students…'* The first librarian was appointed in 1960, when there were 22,000 books in stock and a fund of £800; stock-taking in 1964 revealed the loss of 5,000 items. In 1961 the expanded library was open 9.00am-5.00pm, and to 10.00pm two evenings a week, and two librarians had been appointed. These had grown to five staff by 1969.

Collegiate Hall library in the 1940s

The rapidly increasing student numbers soon put pressure on resources and in 1967 it was reported that the books to students ratio was 18:1, similar to a grammar school (the lowest figure for a university was 70:1). Through the following years, a solution was sought to the desperate need for a new library building and the favoured plan was to build at 35-39 Broomgrove Road; however applications for the compulsory purchase of several houses there were turned down and it became necessary to build on the open space between Main Building and Collegiate Hall. Thus in 1976 the Mary Badland library opened, named after a very supportive HMI.

Southbourne library in the 1940s

Collegiate Learning Centre today

The 1976 Mary Badland library

In 2002 a fine modern extension opened to bring the facilities up to the same quality as the renowned Adsetts Centre at City Campus.

Academic staffing

In 1905, the College opened with six staff. The first staff appointed in addition to Pearson and Henry included a drill instructor, Mr Phipps (two hours a week), teachers of mathematics (Mr Browne) and English (Miss Potter), and a part-time music tutor (Dr Henry Coward). In October 1905 three part-time art teachers arrived - for art (Mr Elliott), plant drawing (Miss Hibberson) and model and object drawing (Mr Carr). Miss Johnson taught French from 1906. The Principal's secretary Miss Campbell Taylor also taught needlework! Another Miss Taylor taught history, helped by Professor Henry Appleton from Sheffield University until 1913. PE for women students started in 1907 under Miss Pigott. Teachers of nature study and chemistry were appointed in 1911 and geography (Mr Tunmer) in 1919.

In 1955 there were still only 27 staff, of whom 11 lived in College, for 349 students.

The 1962 Crescent records teaching staff of 54. By 1968 this had doubled; the total lecturing staff of 113 included 22 Principal Lecturers, 56 Senior Lecturers and 35 Lecturers. The relative importance of subject areas is indicated by staffing levels - 32 in education, 10 each in all branches of science and geography, 12 in art, craft, textiles and handicrafts, eight each in modern languages, physical education and history, six in mathematics, 14 in English, three in music and four in religious education. Staffing rose to about 130 at the time of merger with the Polytechnic in 1976.

In 2003, prior to reorganisation into Faculties, the School of Education had on its staff nearly 100 lecturers (but drawing also on subject specialist expertise from other Schools), 46 administrative and six technical staff, supported by the University central services.

Group photograph, 1955

More detailed group photograph, 1955

55

The College identity

Bowles, Ellis and Herring, students in the 1940s, sporting their blazers

The College was named Sheffield City Training College until 1966 when, as a result of the national Weaver Report, it was renamed Sheffield City College of Education and new articles of governance were introduced. It has from the start developed a strong identity which helped to unite the students and create an active body of alumni. This was probably due partly to the strength of the residential community and of extra-curricular activities such as sport and drama.

The College motto and badge were agreed upon following a competition in 1905. The badge was initially black and gold with lion rampant and a shield charged with eight arrows, but in 1911 the lion and shield were supplemented by a book of knowledge and a crescent designed by E Collington (1910-12). The sheaf and arrows are part of the Sheffield City Coat of Arms. The College blazer, in navy and royal blue with silver, was a good way to display sports achievements and was worn for special events.

Illustration of main building window showing College badge

Crescent magazine cover designs

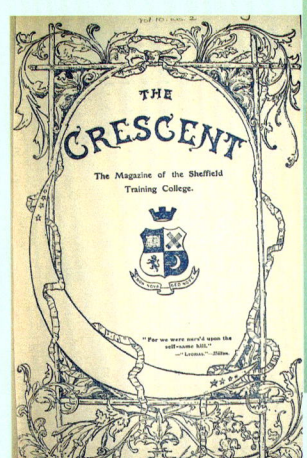

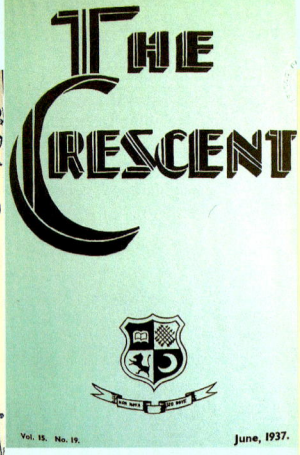

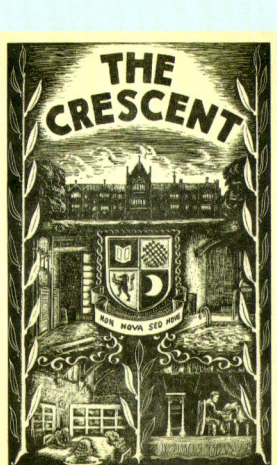

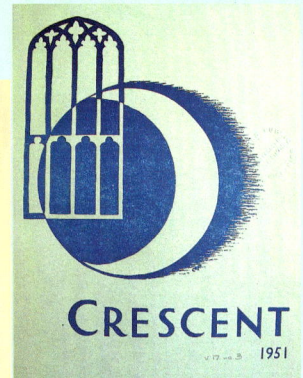

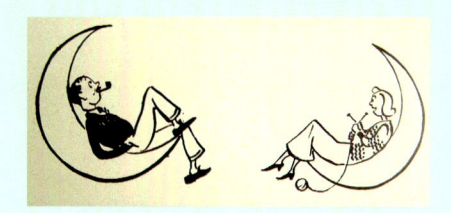

The motto is *'Non nova sed nove'* - *'not new things but in a new manner'* devised by FF Hollas (1905-07).

A quote from the very early days of the College is regularly used in the Crescent magazine:, *'For we were nurs'd upon this self-same hill'* - a line taken from Milton's poem 'Lycidas' written in 1637.

The Crescent magazine, for students and alumni to share their news, express their opinions and put their literary and artistic efforts into print, started to appear monthly in 1905, and then had a varied existence, being followed by termly and then twice-yearly issues to 1942. Through the war it ceased due to paper shortages and then appeared annually from 1946 to 1952, when it merged with the Old Crescenter magazine until the late 1960s.

College blazer and shield

The Crescenters' Association was formed to foster and maintain friendships made at College; alumni groups were very strong at one time and there were several local branches in the 1908-14 period. In 1914-20 activities were curtailed and many groups never met again. Small reunions took place during the years 1920-39, and from 1957 they merged with the Past-Present weekend with many misgivings. In 1952, Old Crescenters had dinner with Mr Wing and Mr Kimbell, accompanied by a dance and a service; in the jubilee year 1955 *'much midnight oil was burnt in the cubicles'*. Over the last few years the reunions of Old Crescenters have occurred over a September weekend.

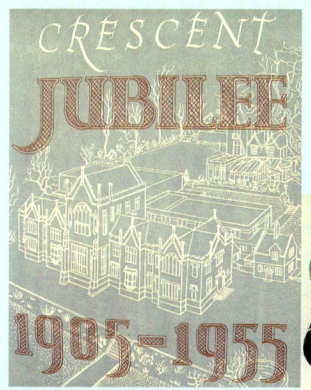

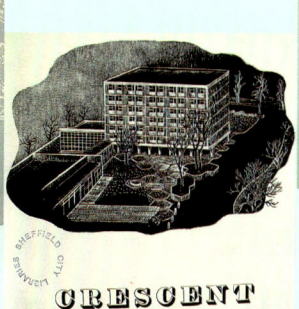

57

Food

The routine for the first 40 years or so of the College did not vary much - the rising bell rang at 7.00am, breakfast of porridge was at 8.00am, lunch was at 12.00 noon, after saying grace, and tea at 5.30pm, with supper at 8.00pm.

In Collegiate Hall the dining hall was on the west side of the Old Head's House. In the 1920s, students sat at tables for 10, each with a prefect to supervise, and 'Mothers' and 'Daughters' sat together (these were paired year one and two students). Tutors were on a raised dais and were joined once a term by Mother/Daughter pairs. Apologies and reasons for lateness had to be given at the top table.

Southbourne had a dining room for 120, to include men from all the smaller residential houses.

Collegiate Hall dining room in the 1940s

Many references to the College catering in the early days are critical. The 1935 inspection found the kitchens antiquated and inadequate, menus not very varied and quantities small, and the *'cost of food per student… so low as to suggest that economy in the supply is being carried to undesirable lengths'*. In the late 1930s, women climbed out of the window of the Brown Room in Collegiate Hall (where smoking was allowed) to get fish and chips on the other side of Ecclesall Road - the shopkeeper allowed them to eat in the back room so that Deputy Principal Daisy Bowker could not see them from her lounge. In the 1940s, students could not eat in the street while wearing a College scarf. Weekend food was worse with items like polony and stewed fruit being served!

During World War Two, the kitchen staff were challenged to feed the students under rationing; the Crescent magazine records, *'major losses on the kitchen front… both our cat and our buns for supper'*. *'When cornflakes melted away, shredded wheat appeared. Syrup ceased but soon there came honey. This very morning the golden (cornflake) age began anew.'* *'Second year men have ceased to complain of the quantity on their plates and argue about food value and vitamin content.'*

The 1955 inspection found that the College had seven dining rooms and kitchens, which lacked leadership and any effective organisation of supplies.

Southbourne dining room in the 1940s

Their recommendations led in 1961 to the opening of a new dining room adjacent to Marshall Hall, to seat 350 - *'meals are now taken by both men and women students in the large new dining room…staff enjoy some measure of privacy…in an alcove off…screened by vivid orange curtains'.* Broomgrove Hall also provided a dining room for 240.

By the 1960s food had improved, with three meals a day provided in the dining rooms, and supper food left in the kitchens on each floor of the halls of residence. *'The next few years will see the rebuilding of a large number of training colleges - let at least their kitchens and dining rooms be made large enough for the new army of teachers, for it seems that our students march on their stomachs!'* (Crescent 1960). But protest continued. One student group in the early 1960s issued a poster depicting the three thinnest students under the heading *'Sheffield Students are Starving!'*

Marshall dining room in the 1960s

By 1967 there were 73 kitchen staff, delivering 1,200 meals and snacks a day. In 1968 a kitchen/dining room extension at Woodville was opened, built by Boot & Son for £37,000, following a review which indicated that a third kitchen and dining room able to provide 350-500 meals was needed. The massive growth in student numbers had been absorbed partly by introducing a cafeteria service.

In the 1980s catered accommodation started to decline and some of the dining rooms were converted to teaching space, leaving only the main dining room with a cafeteria service at Marshall, now known as Millers, and several snack bars around the campus.

Millers today

Money

In 1905 student fees were £10 a year, and the estimated cost of training per student was £21. Teachers' salaries started at £150 a year for male heads, £120 for female heads; male class teachers could earn £90-£220 and female teachers £80-£175. The fee to register with the Teachers Registration Council was one guinea in 1907, and £2 by 1924. Nationally, residential student fees at the time were £53 a year for men and £38 for women.

In the 1920s students paid £45 a year for room, meals, maid service and laundry.

In the late 1930s and early 1940s, each year at college cost £120 (made up of £80 for residence and £40 for tuition). Sheffield Corporation would loan trainees £80 and the Pupil Teacher Centre £40. One student recalled banking £40 a year as a pupil teacher, and paying back the rest at £2 a month for 40 months. Her first salary in 1940 was £162 a year.

In 2005, fees are £1,175 a year (though teacher training attracts many incentives) and a room and catering in Marshall Hall costs £3,285 for 39 weeks accommodation. A newly qualified teacher's salary starts at around £19,000.

Heart of the Campus, Collegiate Crescent

Curriculum

From the opening of the College in 1905, the first Mistress of Method (also called Lady Superintendent) was Mrs Lysbeth Dawson Henry (1856-1946), She had single-handedly run the training of elementary school teachers since 1894 at the Day Training College (since 1891 part of Firth College, later Sheffield University), where she was the first woman member of staff.

Timetables survive from the academic year 1911-1912 showing hour-long lessons in six groups at a time, in mathematics, French, history, English, sewing, science, drill and education, with hygiene, music and drawing saved for the afternoons, and practice on Wednesday afternoons. Initially science was taught at Sheffield University, art at the Art College and drill at the YMCA on the High Street.

Textiles workroom in the building now called Saunders, 1961

In 1918 it was proposed to introduce a new one year Physical Training certificate, as the gym and hostel accommodation were suitable, Sheffield University could teach anatomy and physiology and the PT teacher was highly respected. Initially 30 men were recruited, with a further 65 ex-servicemen taking one term or four term courses. However those who trained on this course were not recognised as qualified teachers and it closed in 1923.

In 1935 an HMI report recorded three distinct courses on offer - advanced, ordinary and short professional - in English, mathematics, history, geography, French, science, music, art, handwork (taken at Psalter Lane), hygiene and PE.

In the 1950s, students were told *'you will teach anything anywhere. We do not certificate prima donnas'*. *'We were trained in steel city, we are true professionals and go on until we drop.'* Priorities changed to two main subjects, one to ordinary and one to advanced level.

Developments in facilities in the 1960s led to the introduction of new subjects: textiles, pottery, woodworking and working with live animals in biology.

Up to the 1960s, training was considered by most to be very intensive and hard work, but unchallenging. However the government drive to turn teacher training into a graduate route led in 1961 to the development of the three year Certificate route, with a fourth year on offer for some leading to the award of a BEd degree; first years were starting to register in 1965.

Student life

During the first fifty years of the College, student life was regimented much like a boarding school; the safe location on the gated estate proved attractive for parents to send their daughters and they were supervised closely. Men and women worked and studied separately, meeting only for dances perhaps once a year.

Among the women, Seniors (second years) became 'mothers' and chose a junior as their 'college daughter' who then occupied their previous year's cubicle and sat with them at meals. This created an early mentor scheme and firm friendships!

Up to 1932, lectures took place from 9.00am to 12.30pm and 2.00 to 4.30pm each weekday, and on Saturday mornings. There was a roll call at each lecture. Students undertook private study in the common room from 6.00pm to 8.30pm with a prefect in charge, prayers and supper were followed by more silent study 8.30-10.00pm and lights out at 10.30pm. Women were not allowed out during the week and had to be back in the hostel by 9.00pm at weekends.

Collegiate Hall, 1941

In the few leisure hours available, activities included trips to the cinema, theatre and concert halls, country dancing, walking in the Peak District, singing in the choral society and drama. The men filled their evenings with *'Smokers'* - games and concerts of songs, music, recitations and speeches. There was no drinking; a bar was not opened on College premises until the 1970s, when it rapidly became a major social hub. Time must have been filled for most by preparing for school practice, participating in societies and sports, and rehearsing for dramatic, choral and operatic performances.

Students sporting College scarves in the 1940s

Students in formal dress in the 1940s

Even Sheffield residents could have only three Saturday nights home a year, and this required a note from parents.

Following the arrival of Ralph Kimbell in 1932, a general relaxation of the rules allowed men and women to mix more. More societies were established. Lectures were 9.00am to 1.00pm daily, and 5.30-7.30pm three evenings a week; students were also expected to do 1.5 hours of private study after 8.00pm.

After World War Two, the men recruits were older, having been in the services, and were paid allowances. The stifling discipline and gender separation started to change.

The big expansion in Dr Wing's time in the 1950s led to further changes; mixed common rooms were opened, a Student Representative Council was formed. The Students' Union had started in 1947 and grew from strength to strength; by 1962 it had a budget of £4,000 and the fee per student was £2. In the 1960s it occupied 17 Broomhall Road until the Pearson building became its home. Students participated enthusiastically in Rag Days.

Student protest, 1976

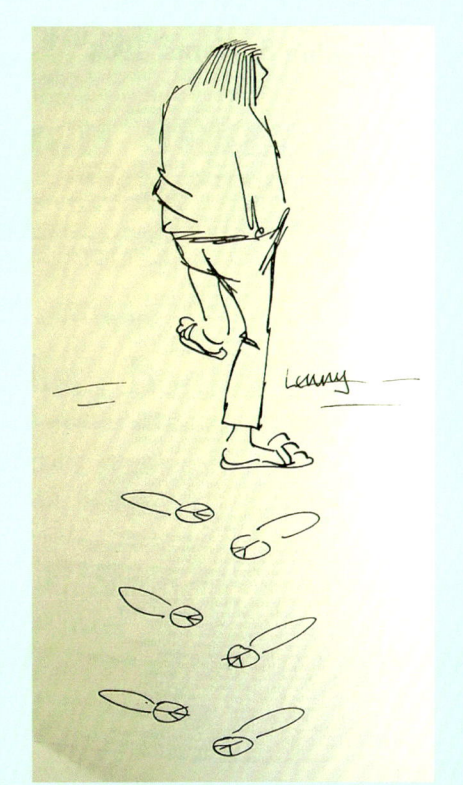

The massive growth in student numbers in the 1960s changed student life for ever; many lived out in lodgings, timetables were staggered to make best use of teaching space, restaurants became cafeteria-style and a bar arrived. The music scene became a key element of College life,

The 1960s and 1970s saw a range of national student protests around such issues as nuclear testing and education cuts. In 1976 there was a three week student occupation of Senior Tutor Constance Gilbey's office in College House and she recalled having to work from her warden flat.

The first mixed halls of residence in the early 1970s proved a positive draw for many applicants.

'Ban the Bomb' cartoon, Crescent magazine

Drama

The College had a strong dramatic society and presented a wide variety of productions both in the College premises - the 1938 assembly hall was well equipped with a stage - and in city venues. Encouraging amateur dramatics no doubt served many purposes for the trainee teacher.

Productions included many Shakespeare plays - *'The Tempest'* in 1955, *'King Lear'* in 1965 and *'Twelfth Night'* in 1933, 1942 and 1948! Other examples of plays put on were Wilder's *'Our Town'* in 1956, Anouilh's *'Ring round the Moon'* in 1962 and Chekhov's *'Cherry Orchard'* in 1968. Often these were reviewed in the Crescent magazine.

Cast of Twelfth Night, 1933

Programme, 1949

There was also an annual Gilbert and Sullivan production by the Operatic Society, such as *'Pirates of Penzance'* in 1937 and *'Princess Ida'* in 1952. However the 1955 Inspection report complained that *'if the College must have operatic performances these could be less frequent and operas by other composers might also be considered!'*

Programmes survive for Lamb's *'Go Down Moses'* in 1945, Sheridan's *'School for Scandal'* in 1949 and Coward's *'Blithe Spirit'* in 1950, among others.

Cast of The Boyfriend, 1975

Performance, 1946-1947

Performance, 1947-1948

Cast of Capek's The Insect Play, 1951

Cast of Iolanthe, 1951

*Leafy Collegiate Campus
from the late 1980s*

Academic developments in the 1980s

The 1980s witnessed contradictory developments for teacher education both nationally and within the Polytechnic. The national demand for new trainee teachers remained low throughout the decade, being just over 19,000 in 1980 and just under 22,000 in 1989, before beginning a steady rise from 1990. In contrast, overall student demand for polytechnic places boomed as government policy kept a lid on the number of university places. The total number of full-time undergraduates in the polytechnics doubled between 1982 and 1992 and in 1991 the polytechnics overtook the universities in the number of full-time undergraduates they enrolled. They also had ten times the number of part-time undergraduates enrolled by the universities (excluding the Open University) in 1992. From playing a very substantial role in post-18 education in the 1960s, Education was by the 1980s contributing under 10 per cent of full-time undergraduate and postgraduate certificate students in British higher education. It was not surprising that some academics in Education, especially those who had experienced the flood-tide of the 1960s and early 1970s, felt their subject was being marginalised.

But there were some points of expansion for Education. To assist Initial Teacher Training providers make the transition required by the massive reduction in student numbers in the late 1970s and early 1980s, the government provided 10,000 to 12,000 full-time equivalent student places each year for in-service training. This corresponded to about one-quarter to one-sixth of their total student teacher training numbers. Alternative forms of study became far more common than ever before. In England and Wales, 6,228 teachers enrolled in 1981-1982 on part-time BEd degrees and 4,901 enrolled on higher degrees. Thousands of teachers engaged in short courses, averaging two days at a time.

These increases offered significant opportunities for the Polytechnic. Extending professional education off-campus and in flexible modes, in consultation with employers, formed an essential part of the Polytechnic's mission. Increased work in in-service education symbolised the switch from full-time residential to a more inclusive, community-based ethos in higher education. Academic staff in the subject departments and in Education developed major initiatives in delivering postgraduate programmes for teachers. One in-service programme of long-term significance was the MSc in Science Education, which sprang from positive collaboration with the Science Faculty. Teachers or lecturers were released for half a day per week; a vital part of the programme was a project in Science supervised by staff from the Science Faculty. The programme provided the basis for applied work which made an inceasingly significant national impact in the 1990s and beyond.

Other departments contributed to part-time postgraduate programmes for teachers which both extended academics' own specialist scholarship and teaching and enhanced teachers' subject understanding and knowledge. An example of wider in-service work came from geography, which had been one of the largest subjects in the former college of education. For a period geography and environmental studies were located at Wentworth Woodhouse, but returned to Collegiate with the establishment of a professional centre in those subjects in the 1980s. The centre provided primary teacher training for BEd and PGCE students and in-service programmes on site and in schools. A number of part-time in-service diplomas flourished, developed in close partnership with LEA advisers. This work was especially aimed at primary teachers lacking subject specialist experience. The centre continued to run short courses in schools and to develop study-packs into the early 1990s, until the tightening of central government funding for in-service training and the lack of prominence of geography in the National Curriculum led to its eventual closure following the retirement of its former head.

Another academic development of considerable importance for the future came from the Polytechnic's department of Education Management. This small group was established in the early 1970s, lodged originally in a foresighted Unit for Management in the Public Services. In 1974 it secured CNAA approval for what was claimed as the first master's degree in Education Management in Europe. The aim was to draw students for the degree from senior managers in schools, LEAs, adult Educational and youth service establishments. Work in this area grew in the 1980s, especially through the provision of an MSc taken by part-time candidates given partial release of time by the LEA. Although changes in government policy in in-service training reduced the group's postgraduate numbers in the early 1990s, academic research and consultancy enhanced the subject's reputation and provided from the late 1990s the basis for renewed expansion and important work in the development of part-time diploma and degree courses in school management.

The early and mid 1980s offered considerable opportunities for innovation. The vast extension of in-service training and education depended upon and flourished within effective partnerships with the LEAs. The Sheffield LEA had made a point of appointing relatively young head teachers of its large comprehensives in the 1970s. Some proved to be inspired leaders and helped create a very positive atmosphere in their schools by the early 1980s. Many teachers found considerable professional fulfilment from extensive curriculum development in the schools. At the same time the new national as well as local emphasis on in-service training recognised that the rapid expansion in the number of teachers in maintained schools between the mid-1960s and the late 1970s had created a profession with sharply different qualifications. Of the 459,000 qualified teachers in England and Wales by 1977, 120,000 were graduates. That showed how far from creating an all-graduate profession the government still was. But among the non-graduate teachers, about 150,000 had been trained for two years, before the non-graduate training course of three years had been introduced in the early 1960s. This diversity of training background had encouraged the government to increase provision for in-service training and explains the variety of professional development opportunities which the Polytechnic was able to work with LEAs and schools to foster.

While the Polytechnic and Education responded to opportunities in the 1980s, there was one worrying legacy from the days of mass expansion in teacher education: the estate acquired by the mergers. Like the original purchase of the Collegiate site, the estate had come together by chance rather than by planning. The expansion of teacher training in the late 1940s had occurred under emergency post-war measures, with government wanting large number of extra teachers quickly and cheaply. Civil servants had got used to requisitioning a variety of buildings, including country houses, during the war for temporary use as training camps, service headquarters, hospitals and so forth. Many country houses had become excessively expensive to run and post-war austerity did not ease matters for their owners, so that houses became available for rent or purchase. Accustomed to packing young adults off to remote rural locations for wartime training or other duties, Whitehall saw an easy way of providing for a short-term need. But with the continuing high demand for new teachers from the 1950s many emergency training centres were made permanent. How it was ever thought that sending trainee teachers off to relatively remote country houses helped prepare them for a working life in a society largely suburban or urban is difficult to understand. Thornbridge and Lady Mabel were especially remote, restricted to women students, and small. Totley, based on a small country house on the edge of Sheffield, accepted both men and women students and had grown to 750 students by 1970. But it was still relatively isolated from city life and the last bus for students in the 1970s was at 10.00pm From the mid-1980s the thrust of Polytechnic policy was to consolidate the number of sites. Decisions to dispose of sites raised complex issues of where departments and faculties might be best located and therefore inevitably stirred controversy. But the new principal, John Stoddart, took the difficult and necessary decision not to continue the lease for Wentworth Woodhouse, where Lady Mabel College had been established in the late 1940s. The college's and then campus' future naturally raised locally significant political concerns in Rotherham, where there was pressure to sustain a post-18 educational establishment in the area and where, in the mid-1980s, there was an acute need to maintain ancillary jobs in a region afflicted by unemployment from the contraction of coal mining and steel production. The insuperable problems for the Polytechnic were the high cost of maintaining the vast country house - maintenance requirements were part of the lease agreement - and the inefficiency of running a small site so far from Sheffield. Consolidation brought important elements of teacher education - physical education and geography/environmental studies - back to Sheffield's main campuses.

As if the massive reduction in trainee numbers and continuing internal re-organisation were not challenges enough, Education faced the Conservative government's initiatives to transform teacher training and the school curriculum. In 1984, the government laid down conditions for courses seeking Qualified Teacher Status. One of them required students to study for a minimum of two years a subject regularly taught in a school and to be instructed in how to teach it to a particular age range. This restricted the range of subject choices within the BEd curriculum. Another condition limited the range of subjects from which PGCE candidates could be taught. A third required teacher educators to possess 'recent and relevant' experience in the classroom.

The 'recent and relevant experience' requirement probably turned out to be less difficult for the polytechnics to meet than it proved irksome and provoking to many university departments of Education. The thinking behind the stipulation was that much teacher training was too remote from classroom experience, too theoretical and, from the Conservatives' perspective, too utopian in its assumptions. The requirement highlighted some real issues about staffing carried over from the College of Education. College lecturer appointments had been heavily based on subject expertise. It has been said by many that the Sheffield City College subject staff saw themselves more as academic experts than as teacher trainers. Former students from the mid-1970s confirm that they felt well taught in the academic subjects but felt far less well prepared for classroom teaching. Part of the problem was the disjunction between lecturers' own professional experience and the nature of the trainees' teaching. Nearly all lecturers at the end of the 1960s were former grammar school teachers, deliberately recruited on the basis of aptitude in their specialist subjects. But the trainees they taught in the academic subjects would proceed to teaching in primary schools and comprehensives. Bruce Oldfield, in his autobiography, noted of the late 1960s that his own experience in grammar school, the *'fairly useless advice'* on classroom teaching he received at college, and the *'struggle'* he had to teach one of his subjects *'at all competently'* made his teaching practice in a secondary school very disillusioning. His was an extreme response by someone who realised that he did not have the nurturing skills needed for successful teaching. But the fact remained that he was not well prepared for teaching widely across the ability range. As late as the early 1980s direct experience of teaching and managing in a comprehensive school was scarce among staff involved in the QTS programmes. Most lecturing appointments had been made, after all, in the period of expansion up to the early 1970s and lecturers appointed had no experience of secondary moderns and little of comprehensives. Most appointees - because of the salaries paid to lecturers - were young, and therefore likely to stay for decades. Meanwhile most secondary education came within the comprehensive system by the early 1970s, and social mores, deeply affecting behaviour in schools, shifted appreciably in the late 1960s and 1970s.

The second national development was the introduction of the National Curriculum, agreed by Parliament in 1988. It prescribed syllabuses for all levels and stages in the schools. For many teachers and lecturers one source of professional stimulus and creativity - in curriculum development, except in the O level and A level years - was removed. Equally important, subjects for study were restricted. One suggested approach to the National Curriculum had been to lay down strict requirements for the core subjects and leave the rest of the teaching time open to schools and teachers to use for subjects as they saw fit. As finally devised, the National Curriculum laid down syllabuses for all subjects and structured the choices of subjects which were offered. This affected subjects' fortunes considerably. geography continued its long-term decline. Among the subjects offered at secondary level at the Polytechnic, physical education also suffered relatively within the new schools curriculum. The creative and performing arts slipped within the national provision for primary education. Design and technology fared well nationally in the balance of the school curriculum and flourishes in the secondary offering in teacher training at Sheffield Hallam University.

By 1990 further changes were unfolding. In 1989 the polytechnics had been removed from local authority control and given independent institutional status. The prospect of the polytechnics becoming universities became a subject of renewed debate. Whether related to this national move for university status or as a separate development, the Polytechnic reorganised its five faculties into twelve schools in 1990. The schools had a vital role in advancing curriculum development and research and ensuring that quality assurance was sustained.

Education became one of the new schools, although many subjects providing specialist expertise remained in other schools. Given the scale of change arising from the National Curriculum and the continuing pace of reform in professional requirements, there was constant pressure within Education to adapt and revise the academic curriculum. Among a variety of initiatives, it is worth mentioning two. A means of stimulating greater interchange between Continuing Professional Development, research, and Initial Teacher Training was provided by the Secondary Education Centre. And the new school fostered a research culture, providing opportunities for more academic staff to register for PhDs than ever before. Personal research had been encouraged in the 1980s and this formed the basis of a more systematic approach to developing research. As with the delivery of teaching, research activity depended upon collaborations across Schools. Research activities and stategies proved highly effective, with Education entering 37 academics in the national Research Assessment Exercise in 1996 and achieving a good result of 3a. The significance of this result, based upon research by staff across the University, was suggested by the facts that no new university secured a higher result and that only three other new universities, all with far fewer staff entered than Sheffield Hallam University, did as well.

The establishment of a School of Education occurred in the context of renewed national demand for teachers. In 1980 the national intake of initial teacher trainees had been just over 19,000. In 1988 it just over 20,000. Big increases occurred from autumn 1990. Demand peaked at 32,000 in 1992 and stayed at around 29,000 new entrants in the next three years. Expansion affected primary and secondary about equally. The Polytechnic shared in this recovery. Between merger in 1976 and 1981 the total number of teacher trainees fell from 1,820 to 800 students in all years. It slipped to 760 in 1986, the level of demand experienced 25 years earlier. By 1992 its trainee numbers had bounced back to 1,327 in all years. The revival of recruitment underpinned the rationale for a separate School of Education.

One threat to this revival arose from the Conservative government's interest in moving the locus of training increasingly into the schools. The shift to the one-year PGCE as the main route into teaching had occurred in the 1970s. An ideological disposition to distrust theory over practice and a conviction that Educationalists were predominantly left of centre politically led the government to foster trials involving increased training of teachers in the schools. By the end of 1991 a review of those trials indicated that the experiment was not going well. Training teachers in schools was costing three times more than the original estimates and more than the traditional one-year PGCE. The experiment depended on consortia between higher education trainers, schools and the LEAs, with the last often proving the least firmly committed to the partnerships. Schools found the workload far heavier and more time-consuming than they had initially anticipated; they had difficulties in supplying cover for teachers involved in the in-school training; and their teachers sought more training themselves than had been predicted initially. But, in addition to these pressures on costs and time, it was also found that trainees wanted more theory to underpin their practice and more time in an academic setting to reflect upon their experiences in the classroom. The first director of the School of Education, Professor Asher Cashdan, publicly agreed that more training in schools was desirable, but stressed the need for academic input, adding that learning theory was *'probably more important'* than teaching theory in preparing trainees. The government would soon return to the issue of training in schools.

At the time when the polytechnics acquired university status in 1992, the trend of developments was to reverse at least some of the effects of the dispersal which had occurred after merger. Education's significance within the institution revived with the revival of student numbers. The provision of courses and degrees for Continuing Professional Development, central to the Polytechnic's mission, had expanded for Education out of all recognition since the mid-1970s. Research within Education, or related to Education, had grown far beyond the scholarly and very limited research activity undertaken in Sheffield City College. And, although many groups contributing to teacher education remained in other Schools, there was a far stronger organisational focus for teacher training than there had been at any time since 1976.

William Brookfield
1809-1874

Friend of Alfred Lord Tennyson, William Henry Brookfield was the son of the solicitor, Charles Brookfield, who lived at Southbourne. While at Trinity College, Cambridge, William befriended members of the secret society, 'the Cambridge Apostles', who later became well-known literary figures such as Thackeray, Carlyle, Hallam and Tennyson; he remained part of their circle throughout his life. *'Old Brooks, as Tennyson called him, was the funniest of men… he could make a whole roomful of them roll around on the floor with laughter'* (Levi 1993). Tennyson is thought to have visited the family at Southbourne. William married writer Jane Octavia Elton; he once wrote to his wife from the house, calling it *'South Borneo, Schewild'*.

William Brookfield became a school inspector in 1848; he held several parish appointments, as well as being canon of St Paul's in London and honorary chaplain to the Queen. His son Charles Hallam Elton Brookfield (1857-1913) became a famous playwright.

Canon Brookfield died in Chelsea in 1874. Tennyson wrote a sonnet to his memory starting:

'Brooks, for they call'd you so that know you best…
Old Brooks, who loved so well to mouth my rhymes…'

Portrait of William Henry Brookfield, in the late 1840s by Sir Anthony Coningham Sterling, now in the National Portrait Gallery

Some original Tennyson manuscripts and letters were discovered in the Paradise Square offices of solicitors Gould & Coombe many years later.

Sir William Christopher Leng
1825-1902

One of Collegiate Crescent's most prominent residents was Sir William Leng. Born in Hull in 1825, he was writing for the Dundee Advertiser by 1859. His brother Sir John was MP for Dundee and a newspaper proprietor. Leng came to Sheffield in 1864 as part proprietor of the *Sheffield Telegraph*, which gave him the opportunity to *'write as he felt'*.

He bought Oaklands (see item about Oaklands) in 1879 from a solicitor, William Fennell. The house had been built in 1849. Leng lived there until his death in 1902, after which Annie Lubbock Leng was in residence. His son Christopher attended the Collegiate School, and later took over as proprietor of the newspaper from his father.

Oaklands was a fine house with a pleasure garden to the north; Leng also bought 40 Collegiate Crescent which he leased out, either as an investment or to protect his privacy.

Leng was described as *'constitutionally combative'*, *'loves a fight'*, *'gives hard, very hard blows'*. He was a *'complete master of satire'*. *'He has made Sheffield Conservatism and in Ecclesall he is practically dictator'* (Sheffield Weekly News 9 September 1899). *'Sir William smokes and works. He does nothing else.'* He earned his knighthood through stamping out rattening - workers' sabotaging of equipment to enforce the interests of trade societies in the local grinding trades - in Sheffield through a Parliamentary enquiry.

SIR WILLIAM LENG.

Sir William Leng, Sheffield Weekly News, *Notes and Queries, 1899*

Annie Jennings (Thomas)
1884-1999

Annie was one of the first intake of students to the College in 1905 and lived to become the oldest person in Britain. She was born in 1884 in Wales. She is pictured in a group of women on the steps of Main Building. She came to only the second college in England to be opened following the 1902 Education Act, and one of only four colleges admitting both men and women. In 1905 she may have been one of the 27 women who lodged in the Old Head's House at the centre of Collegiate Hall (before the wings were built) under the supervision of Deputy Superintendent Mrs Lysbeth Henry. The other 35 women and 28 men who also started in 1905 would have lived at home or lodged with families. At that time there were 10 staff, several part-time. Annie's fees were £10 a year, and she would have done some of her studying in rented rooms at Carver Street Wesleyan Chapel and in the science laboratories at Sheffield University.

Female staff and students, 1905

She recalled visiting France in 1909 and seeing Bleriot's flight across the Channel - *'I came out of college and I didn't have any money, and father said, 'Never mind I'll give you the money'. He was a very wise and kind man... I was late going to college because my birthday is in November.'*

In the mid 1920s she was Miss Thomas, head of North Wingfield Infants School and she also taught at Hipper Street School. She married a Clay Cross curate, Louis Jennings, who died in the 1940s of blackwater fever; they had no children. Annie reached her 115th birthday before her death in November 1999, making her the oldest person in Britain. She lived alone at Wingerworth, and was remembered as a reclusive, but bright and independent woman, with a tremendous sense of humour and great agility, who attended church up to the age of 109 and recovered from a broken leg at 110! In her obituaries, it is recalled *'Many... combined almost a fear of her with deep affection... I imagine in her days as a head teacher even the school inspector trod carefully!'*

Annie, 1905

Annie in later life

Stainless Stephen
1891-1971

One of the most popular radio entertainers of the 1930s, Arthur Clifford Baynes was born in May 1891 in Sheffield. He trained at Sheffield City Training College in 1910-12, where he specialized in psychology (said to help him later to understand his audiences!), participated in drama productions, and captained the swimming team.

He started teaching in the West Riding in 1912, and in World War One served in the York and Lancaster Regiment; having been wounded twice, he trained in signalling and got the idea from telegrams for his famous comedy act of punctuating his jokes with commas, full-stops and semi-colons! He was able to practice by entertaining the troops with mimicry and comic bulletins.

In 1922 he took a teaching post at Crookes Endowed School where he remained until 1935.

His first stage appearance in Luton in 1921 was followed by his radio debut on Sheffield Relay Station in 1924. He specialised in after-dinner speaking and one-man pantomimes; relying on topical issues from the newspapers, and research on people's characteristics, he made sport of people but was never offensive. His stage name was Stainless Stephen - suggestive of Sheffield, his nickname Stainless was given to him as a teenager with a new bike. On stage he wore a bowler hat, white tie and a stainless steel waistcoat made by Firth Vickers. He worked in the school holidays, and in the evenings, driving himself endless miles in a Jaguar. The boys at school were his best critics.

Will's cigarette card of Stainless Stephen

By 1932 he topped a poll to find the most popular national radio artist and featured on a cigarette card. In the 1930s he starred as the judge in the Flitch Trials, a competition to pick a happily married couple to win a flitch of bacon, which ran in City Hall in November 1935. In World War Two he worked with ENSA to entertain the troops, giving over 100 shows around the world.

He retired to a farm in Kent in 1956 and died in 1971, describing himself as *'Stainless Stephen - fameless, aimless, brainless, shameless, painless Stephen now approaching semi-dotage - semicolon!'*

Music and Sir Henry Coward

Music has played a big part in life on the 'Crescent', even in the Victorian era. Soon after the first houses were built, Baron James Wehli leased Oakdale at 36 Collegiate Crescent (now College House) from 1860-64 for £145 a year. He was an internationally renowned composer; there are 15 of his compositions listed among American sheet music between 1870 and 1885. He was also a professional pianist and established an orchestra in Sheffield, but it was not successful and he left in 1864. *'The town revealed an aloofness characteristic of it in those times and refused to honour him.'* He had played for Queen Victoria and other royalty (Stainton 1924). A lease for the house dated 1866, just after he left, includes an inventory and there were pianos in the drawing room, library, dining room, dressing room and landing!

From its foundation the College had a strong tradition of music, mainly due to the influence of gifted individuals. The first music master was Sir Henry Coward (1849-1944). A former cutlery apprentice at Washington Works, he began teaching singing classes and then became a pupil teacher, rising quickly to the headship of an elementary school, leaving that post in 1887. After gaining an Oxford B.Mus in 1889 and being one of very few to gain a Mus.Doc in 1894, he taught part-time at the College from 1905 to 1920, and also at Sheffield University, King Edward VII School and the High School. One pupil teacher attending the Normal Day Training Department recalls his lessons in a room above a bookshop on Church Street where *'he trained us in his beloved tonic sol-fa methods… and in his zeal and energy would pick up the iron poker from the hearth and beat time on the desks'*.

He composed many choral and orchestral works, cantatas such as *'Magna Charta'* and *'The Story of Bethany'*. He conducted nine bands and choirs for Queen Victoria's visit in 1897 when she opened the Town Hall, and conducted the Sheffield Festival chorus at the opening of the University in 1905. He is best known for founding what became the Sheffield Musical Union in 1876, probably England's leading amateur chorus (*'frivolous choristers tremble when they catch the gleam in his eye'*), and conducting it for 57 years until he retired in 1933. This became the Sheffield Philharmonic Chorus in 1935 and is still performing, often in City Hall. In 1911 Coward undertook a six-month world tour with the choir. He was knighted in 1926 and died at his home at 6 Kenwood Road.

Coward must have been largely responsible for establishing the College's Choral Society, which thrived throughout its history. During and beyond the time of Principal Ralph Kimbell (1932-49), who had a degree in music and conducted the Choral Society at Durham prior to joining the College, the following were performed by the College students.

1937   *Mass in B Minor (Bach)* at City Hall
Pied Piper (Parry)
For the Fallen (Elgar)
1938   *Creation (Haydn)* at Victoria Hall
Messiah (Handel)
1941   *St Matthew Passion (Bach)*
Mass in E flat (Schubert)
1942   *St Paul (Mendelssohn)* in Victoria Hall
My Spirit was in Heaviness (Bach)
Blest Pair of Sirens, The Glories of our Blood and State (Parry)
1951   *Jesu Priceless Treasure (Bach)* in Sheffield Cathedral
1952   *Benedicite (Vaughan Williams)*
Ode to Music (Parry)
1955   *Imperial Mass (Haydn)*
Pianoforte Concerto in D
1956   *Passion according to St John*

Sir Henry Coward, Sheffield Weekly News, Notes and Queries, 1899

Dr Wing was also an accomplished musician and he and his family played in the College orchestra. In Southbourne *'early rising was facilitated by the Wings' early morning cello and violin sessions'* (Crescent 1952).

Music was a strong subject on the curriculum until the mid 1970s, despite the College never having very suitable teaching and practice space. The 1955 inspection reported that there was only *'one grand piano, and many of the upright pianos are in need of attention… more electric gramophones are needed'*. There were about 35 students of music (out of 349) across the two years and *'all players are encouraged to join the orchestra which is inevitably unbalanced and lacking in quality'*. This compares to 130 out of 202 taking a music course in 1935, when all students spent an hour a week choral singing.

The College had a thriving operatic group who put on an annual Gilbert and Sullivan performance. Jazz became very popular in the late 1950s with a weekly jazz club, and bands known as the Crescent Jazzmen or the Sheaf River Jazzmen. In the 1960s, a thriving folk club was established. Dances were held regularly; in the early days, the annual dance was the only time that the male and female students met! In the late 1960s, fashion designer Bruce Oldfield was chair of the social committee and organised the bands for the popular weekly dances in the dining room behind Marshall.

College Principals

One of the strengths of the College was its leadership, with the continuity derived from long-serving Principals (only five over its 70 years), and some very strong Deputy Principals such as Lysbeth Henry (1905-1922), Daisy Bowker (1933-1948) who went on to become Principal of Thornbridge College, Jane Moulton (1948-1967) awarded an OBE for her services to education, David Bradshaw (1968-1970) who became Principal of Doncaster College, and Brian Cane (1970-1976).

Three Deputy Principals, 1955

The first Principal was The Reverend Valentine Ward Pearson (1857-1930) who served from the opening of the College in 1905 through the difficult years of new building and World War One, until he retired to Anglesey in 1921. He was formerly chaplain and head of Wesley College, with which the Grammar School merged in 1905.

Jane Moulton with Dr Peake at her retirement party, 1967

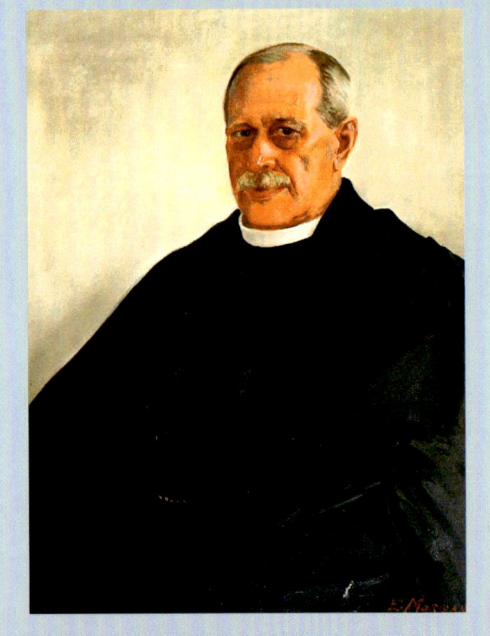

He was remembered as *'firm yet kindly and his students loved him. His Christian ideals and way of life carried him forward and without doubt left their mark on his students...'* (Crescent 1955).

Principal Pearson

He was followed by Samuel Hoole (1871-1960), Principal from 1921 to 1932. He had been Principal of Sunderland Day Training College prior to coming to Sheffield.

He was succeeded in 1932 by Ralph Kimbell (died 1964) who trained and taught at Culham College, and had been Vice Principal of the College of the Venerable Bede at Durham. Known as 'Prinny', he was said to be an aloof character who demanded respect. He was a gifted musician and gave musical recitals on Tuesday evenings.

Kimbell had to steer the College through the challenging years of World War Two. During a long illness, Mrs 'Prinny' Kimbell wrote many letters to students in the forces and put their photos on the music room wall as a 'Rogues Gallery'; Mr Kimbell created booklets from their news which were circulated.

Principal Hoole

He believed strongly in co-education, *'citizens living along Ecclesall Road were shocked to see evidence of loss of discipline, for the women students walked and talked openly with the men…'*

On retirement in 1949, he took holy orders and became a curate in Herefordshire.

Principal Kimbell

College Principals

The next Principal was Dr Herbert Dennis Wing from 1949 to 1965 (died 1968). After being Deputy Principal of Newlands Park Training College, and Principal of Burderop Park Training College at Swindon, he led the College through the years of extremely rapid expansion until he retired in 1965. Wing and his family were skilled musicians and played in the College Orchestra.

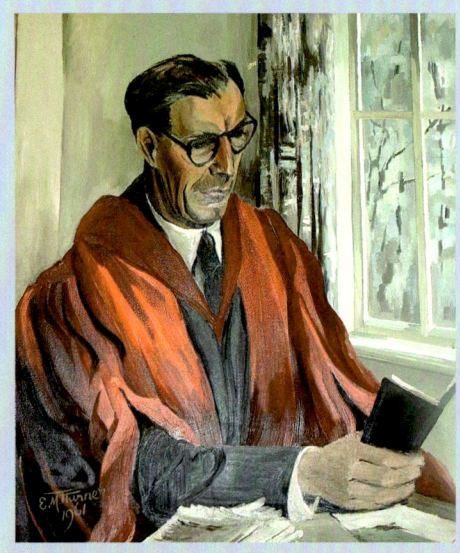

Principal Wing

Wing took the College through a trebling of student numbers, building new halls of residence (*'to a pre 1960 student... the scene must be virtually unrecognisable. In place of the cloistered atmosphere... now sprawls the vast Wing empire.'*) and refurbishing teaching space. He *'was a man with vision and purpose'*. He made many innovations - he favoured increasing day training students, prioritised the provision of social space, and reviewed the curriculum and staff ability to deliver it.

Drawing of Principal Wing

In September 1955 three Principals - Hoole, Kimbell and Wing - joined the Jubilee celebrations and took part in a service in College Hall.

The last College Principal was Dr Harry Peake, from 1965 until the College merged with Sheffield City Polytechnic in1976. A physicist and mathematician, Peake had worked in government intelligence at Bletchley during World War Two, was head of Bilborough Grammar School in Nottingham, and taught at Loughborough College of Technology prior to coming to Sheffield.

Three principals - (left to right) Wing, Hoole and Kimbell, 1955

Principal Peake

Mabel Leather and support staff

An extremely interesting and different view of College life is given by a former maid at Collegiate Hall. Mabel Leather was born in 1913, one of 13 children, on Moore Street. She attended the High School at Greystones, and might have progressed to office work but for a period of illness, which interrupted her schooling. Aged 15 in 1928, she started as a corridor maid at Collegiate Hall, initially being paid six shillings (30p) a week, which she handed over to her mother, receiving back two shillings and six pence (12.5p). By the age of 21, she was earning 16 shillings (80p) a week.

In Collegiate Hall alone, there were three kitchen maids, three dining maids, two dormitory maids, two tutors' maids, two corridor maids, and a maid each for the Deputy Principal Miss Bowker and Matron Miss Hawkins. The Cook was Mrs Bennett.

The maids lived two or three to a room in the attics of the central 'island' (former head's house) beside the sick bay, and ate in the service room next to the kitchen. As corridor maid, Mabel had to keep the eest wing corridors and bathrooms clean; she never worked in the east wing nor visited the other College buildings. Later she was promoted to third maid, then head maid, in the dining room. The maids became close and lifelong friends, but despite being of the same generation did not become friendly with the students.

Mabel Leather outside Collegiate Hall library windows where she fell

Mabel as a young woman

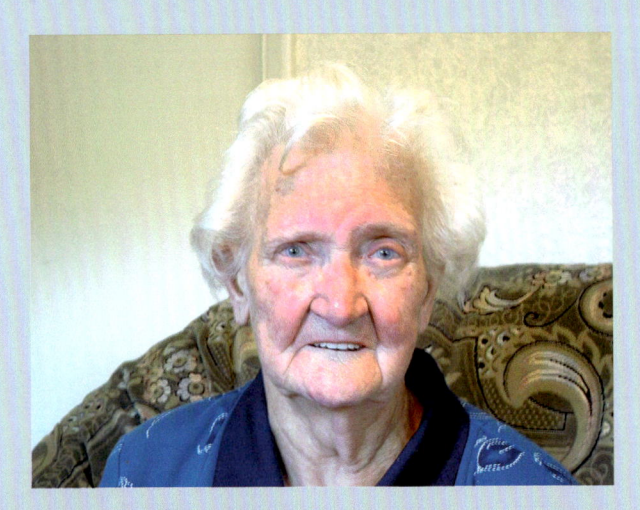

Mabel's uniform was blue and white in the morning, and she changed to black and white for lunch; the College provided large morning aprons and small afternoon aprons, which went to the laundry, and caps with black velvet bands. She had to provide her own black uniform. At one point cream linen blinds were replaced with curtains and put in cupboards for many years; she made several suits out of them!

Her day started at 6.30am; the maids ate their breakfast and lunch after the students. Packed sandwiches were provided for those going out on teaching practice. She recalls the food being mainly

Mabel today

roast meat, with fish on Fridays. High tea was at 5.00-6.00pm, after which the maids could have a few hours' free time on a rota - Mabel often used to catch a tram or bus to the edge of Sheffield and walk back across the moors. Supper was provided in the service room about 9.00pm and lights out at 10.00pm.

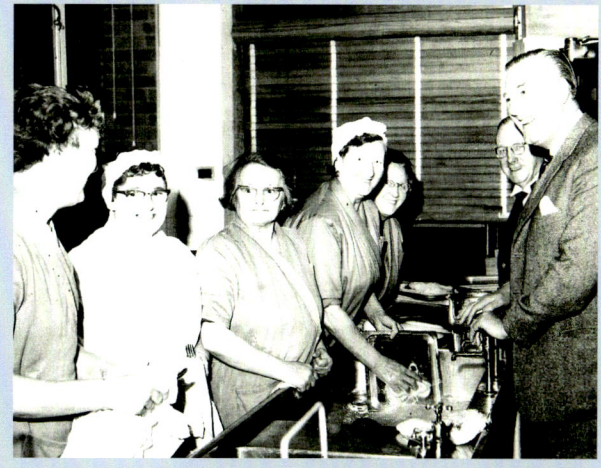

She was initially given one half day off a week, later changed to Saturday teatime to Sunday teatime, when she was allowed to go home overnight. She often went to the cinema or theatre. In her two weeks' paid holiday, she usually stayed on a farm and went walking in Derbyshire.

She recalls queueing outside Matron's store to be issued with cleaning materials. Matron gave her daily doses of cod liver oil and malt, and Parish's chemical food till she was 21. One vacation, she was cleaning the high transoms of the library windows, when the ladder slipped and she fell and cut her face badly. She had her nose stitched by a local doctor, and was taken to the Royal Infirmary. She received £10 compensation.

Catering staff meet the Minister of Education, Sir David Eccles, in 1961

At the end of each term, she would arrange to send the girls' trunks by horse and dray to the station, which cost 1 shilling (5p).

Mabel never met the Principal and there were no men working at Collegiate Hall, other than one boiler man. After the annual dance, she was posted as guard at the bottom of the stairs to the dormitories to ensure no male visitors slipped upstairs!

Household staff seated at table in Collegiate Hall

Mabel worked at the College for 10 years - she joined the Land Army in 1939.

When Mabel left in 1939, there was a medical officer, two clerical assistants, 30 domestic servants, a caretaker, a laboratory helper, three cleaners and five gardeners/grounds men (Education Committee Report 1939).

The 1962 Crescent records the appointment of the first two librarians. A new post of lodgings officer was created in 1966. In 1967 there were 116 domestic staff, 73 kitchen staff and two sewing room staff, seven caretakers and six ground staff; there were no repairs or maintenance staff and it was proposed to hire some. The role of matron was renamed bursar. By 1969 10 porters and three technicians had been hired, and there were 12 administrative and clerical staff and five library staff.

Alderman Marshall, JP
1890-1981

For over 40 years the College benefited from the committed support of Alderman Samuel Hartley Marshall, who played a significant part in the life of the College. He was an insurance agent, JP and councillor for Attercliffe for many years, Lord Mayor of Sheffield in 1943 and elected an Alderman in 1945. He was made an honorary Freeman of the City in 1965 at a ceremony in City Hall, in recognition of his contribution to the life of Sheffield.

Alderman Marshall chaired the Training of Teachers Sub-Committee from 1946 to 1967. He felt that *'knowing the people and knowing the place'* were of supreme importance - he attended formal events, concerts and plays, and visited the kitchens and common rooms (Crescent 1967). The College honoured him by naming its first new hall of residence built in 1960 Marshall Hall after him.

Alderman Marshall at the 1955 College jubilee celebrations

Bruce Oldfield

Renowned fashion designer Bruce Oldfield trained to be a teacher at the College, specialising in art and craft.

Born in 1950, son of a Jamaican boxer, he was raised partly in a Barnardo's home in Ripon and partly by a foster mother who was a dressmaker and developed his interest in designing clothes. After attending Ripon Grammar School, he joined the College in 1968. In his autobiography *'Rootless'* (2004), he confided he found out very quickly he was *'not cut out to be a teacher'*, that teaching was *'terrifying'* and he was not *'the nurturing type'*. In 1969 he became chair of the social committee and organised all the College dances and discos, as well as discovering his talent for making and selling items of clothing. By the time he left Sheffield he had *'gained enormously in confidence... something that has been incredibly valuable... ever since. And with self-esteem came ambition.'*

Following his years in Sheffield, he attended Ravensbourne College of Art in 1971-1972 and then St Martins, starting his own fashion house in 1975. Since his early designs for Charlotte Rampling, he has created fashions for royalty and many celebrities such as Joan Collins and Joanna Lumley.

Bruce Oldfield in his student days

Sheffield City Polytechnic awarded him an Honorary Fellowship in 1987, and he was appointed an OBE in 1990 for services to fashion and industry.

Collegiate Campus buildings, 1970

Re-alignments

The 1990s saw the working through of two new developments. The School of Education was formed in 1990 as part of the Polytechnic's re-organisation following the securing of autonomy from the local authority and, as it then happened, preparatory to university status. This coincided with the renewed national demand for trainee teachers flowing from the rise in the birth-rate. Between 1988 and 1992 the number of ITT entrants rose by 50 per cent. Sheffield Hallam University, as it became in 1992, shared fully in that growth. Its total ITT numbers rose from 800 or fewer in the early and mid 1980s to 1327 in 1992. But the raw numbers of new trainees disguised various shifts. It has already been noted that the PGCE became the main training pathway by the late 1970s. The Conservative government sought to channel as much trainee time as possible into school practice and through Circular 14/93 in late 1993, the Department for Education increased the time required in school practice. Under the Education Act of 1994, the new Teacher Training Agency acquired the power to fund teacher education based entirely within schools and a number of school partnerships arose to provide teacher education.

This increased time spent by trainees in schools had a number of consequences. The time available on campus was so reduced that parts of the curriculum were dropped. This affected the study of the history, philosophy, sociology and psychology of education. While many within teacher education agreed that some of these subjects may have become detached from the practice of teaching, there seems little rationale for sustaining a national approach to teacher education which omits any sustained examination of child and educational psychology. The remaining part of the curriculum which concentrated on Professional Courses divided into work on classroom presentation techniques and a range of more specialist applied courses. Those courses were also sub-divided by students' choice of the age-range they preferred to teach: first school, middle school, or secondary school. This strand provided the base for much curriculum development in the 1990s, with modules being developed in particular aspects of pedagogy and in such specialisms as Special Educational Needs. The national thrust of educational policy went against approaches fostered for decades. For example, when the Plowden report on primary school teaching methods appeared in 1967 a lecture was given at College to emphasise that Sheffield was already on the track endorsed by Plowden. That approach was to foster group projects in primary schools and give greater emphasis to linking all subjects by, for instance, taking a topic and considering its context from various disciplinary angles. Such an approach fitted in well with methods adopted in West Riding schools under its innovative Chief Education Officer, Alec Clegg. In English, the most heavily subscribed single teaching subject in the College, David Mattam was a charismatic lecturer whose teaching and writing underscored the importance of what the pupil/student wrote rather than spelling and grammar as ends in themselves. By the mid and late 1970s spider diagrams proliferated and flow charts spread. Subject integration and focus on topics dominated much curriculum planning and delivery. These were not approaches that fitted the assumptions behind the National Curriculum.

The second consequence was that schools were now paid by teacher trainers for the work they put into mentoring trainees. Providers retained substantially less funding per trainee and this financial blow coloured universities' attitudes towards the financial impact of expanding ITT and the potential instability of funding received from ITT. Given the government's record on allocating numbers in the 1980s, many universities decided to limit their commitment to teacher training. A further development compounded these shifts. A number of institutions decided to reduce the undergraduate degree from four to three years. Sheffield Hallam University followed that trend. That decision, together with the reduction in the amount of trainees' time spent on campus, meant that, while entry numbers rose, the amount of teaching provided on campus did not grow in proportion. The revival of demand for trainees in the 1990s did not, therefore, lead to an equivalent resurgence in Education as a subject.

National demand certainly proved effervescent. The total of nearly 32,000 new ITT entrants in 1992 fell back to around 29,000 in each of the three years 1993 to 1995 and then slipped further to 25,500 to 27,000 in 1998 to 2000 inclusive. Sheffield Hallam University's total ITT numbers fell even more steeply from 1,382 in 1995 to 1,054 by 2000, reflecting in part the impact of reducing the course length from four to three years in undergraduate routes. The disproportionate reduction also reflected the impact of the TTA's method of allocating cuts in numbers on the basis of Ofsted quality ratings. While primary ranked as a category B provider - a good rating - five out of the nine secondary subjects by 1998 were category C providers, though that went down to two in 1999. When reduced numbers were allocated, higher category providers were protected.

By 2000, the new entrants at Sheffield Hallam University totalled 636, with 334 being in secondary and the others in primary. Two-thirds of secondary entrants and under half primary entrants were PGCE. Some 56 per cent of the secondary entrants were male, partly because of the mix of subjects, in stark contrast to 11 per cent of primary entrants. A clear majority of the secondary trainees (59 per cent) were 25 years or older on entry, while very nearly half the primary trainees were of that age. Primary consistently recruited five per cent or less of its new students from minority ethnic groups. In the late 1990s a substantially higher proportion of primary PGCE entrants had a 2:1 or better degree than did entrants to the secondary PGCE. While this might, again, reflect the subject mix, because it has been more difficult to recruit highly qualified graduates in the shortage subjects, the need for a strong academic record in a specific subject would seem more necessary at the secondary than at the primary level. The prior level of attainment of secondary trainees also suggests that secondary teachers need far more long-term support in subject knowledge enhancement than policy makers seem to accept. The belated national recognition of this need for science teachers bore fruit in 2002-2003 in a major DfES - Wellcome Trust initiative in which the Centre for Science Education at Sheffield Hallam University played a leading role. The National Science Education Centre and its regional centre will provide extensive subject enhancement for science teachers and support staff in schools.

National intake in teacher training: peaks and troughs, 1988-2003

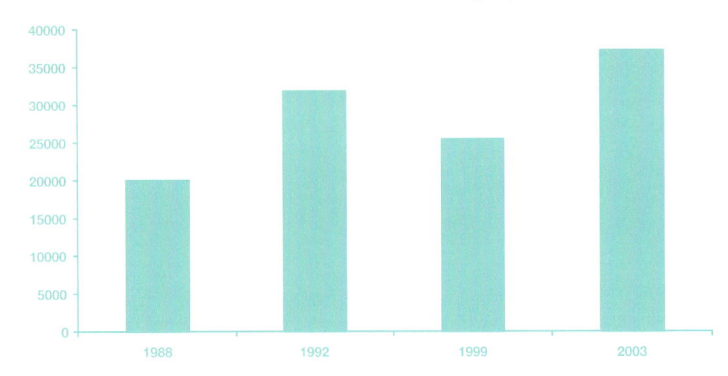

In terms of organisation, the School of Education expanded its remit in the 1990s. On its formation it incorporated all primary and all aspects of professional training. But of the nine specialist subjects taught in secondary, four lay outside the School. Mathematics joined in 1997 and science followed a few years later. Design and technology and physical education remained outside the School and indeed the new Faculty. This very unusual arrangement has not impeded the successful development of those two subjects. The School also grew by hosting new programmes in counselling and in early childhood studies, by becoming the base for TESOL, and by promoting the development of the study of autism. In some ways the organic growth of subjects within the School of Education prefigured the concentration on the whole child which is now being more formally organized in schools.

The main objections to the overwhelming emphasis on practice in teacher training range widely. Many argue that the whole purpose of training is to give all those involved in it an opportunity to reflect upon what they are doing, challenge orthodoxy, and take at least some time to relate developing and contended theory to practice-based research. Many trainees would welcome the opportunity to spend more time between teaching practices to evaluate and reflect upon their experiences. In terms of public perceptions of schooling, there has been a consistent view throughout the 1980s and 1990s that the best way to improve schools is by providing smaller-sized classes and better-quality teachers. Yet research on students' performance in GCSE indicates that the single variable which most affects attainment is social class. Once individual schools enrol significant proportions of poorer pupils (an early study suggested 30 per cent) average GCSE scores fall. And within schools, extremes of affluence and poverty shape results.

Such conclusions have led to various interventions in schools returning GCSE results well below average. Some interventions have emphasized the importance of varying the nature of pupils' work, with more time spent in placements, employment-related activity, and contact with adults who might offer role-models or support figures outside the home. Studies undertaken for LEAs at Sheffield Hallam University emphasise the generally positive effects of such structured interventions. Pupils themselves feel increasingly involved in their learning and more confident of their capacity to acquire skills or knowledge. Teachers, if supported by staff development and effective administration, become more empowered. Such local studies fit well with research which stresses that pupils' performance in primary schools of similar demographic features in poorer neighbourhoods improve if the teachers in a school work effectively as a group. That in turn raises issues about the role and impact of school leadership which has been a focus of postgraduate teaching and research at Sheffield Hallam University since the 1970s. The School of Education was therefore well placed to meet increasing interest within the school system from the 1990s in management and leadership development. It expanded its provision of courses in those areas.

Throughout teaching, from the trainee to the headteacher, practice needs to be informed by reflection and research. From the 1990s the School of Education both responded to external opportunities to extend its engagement with CPD and pressed for more systematic approaches to career-long CPD for teachers. Part of that thrust has been in enhancing teachers' understanding of issues raised by the pursuit of organizational excellence. Part has involved providing courses meeting specific training needs, perhaps most notably in ICT applications.

Working with ICT in the schools has attracted major local initiatives but remains challenging nationally. The most recent national survey of NQTs' reflections upon their training during their first year in teaching records that one aspect of training which NQTs continue to find least effective is their preparation to use ICT in the classroom. Although 57 per cent rated their preparation as good or very good, this was a low level of satisfaction and indicated that a very significant minority of NQTs felt under-prepared. When defining what constituted an effective teacher was raised (or provoked) by Ofsted in the late 1990s, the Teacher Training Agency responded in 1999 by spelling out 50 skills and understandings which trainees needed to demonstrate before securing Qualified Teacher Status.

The problem with this approach is that different skills are involved in teaching with ICT and they develop at different rates. Trainee teachers need support at different times according to their professional development needs and in relation to their own reflection of their students' learning. The integration of trainees' understanding, their students' capacity to learn, their students' pace of learning, and ICT methodologies is far more important to the effective application of ICT than a focus simply on enhancing trainees' technical expertise. Given the complexity of this process of assimilation and application, the obvious question arises as to why this highly challenging aspect of practitioner skill, about which successive cohorts of trainees register their unease, has to be secured with the ITT programme. This rapidly changing part of teaching methodology could surely be an important element in a structured programme of in-service professional development during the first four or five years of teaching.

The main criticism of external expectations of teacher training is that it ignores the range and complexity of the issues arising from pedagogy and subject development. The role of major university centres for teacher training is to probe and re-evaluate such issues. It is hardly unimportant, for example, that 50 per cent of children at 16 years fail to meet minimum targets in national tests in mathematics. To redress that level of under-achievement may require a major shift in how secondary mathematics is taught, in terms of focusing on thinking and understanding key concepts, and of providing learning materials with which pupils are more ready to engage. This extent of student shortfall is not demonstrably related to teachers' lack of effectiveness in using ICT or their uncertain awareness of issues endemic in a multicultural society, or their ignorance of the challenges facing commerce and industry. The methods of teaching and the ways in which mathematical concepts are presented are more fruitful areas through which to attempt to tackle under-attainment. In addressing issues of pedagogy, the obvious retort to those who suspect that proffered solutions are based on modish or 'politically' inspired prejudices, is that student teachers need to be equipped to read and evaluate the relevant research literature and to test and reject methods which their own professional experience suggest are inapplicable. Their professional training needs to be rigorous enough to ensure that they possess the skills, theoretical understanding, and methodological expertise to evaluate what they have learned. Only intellectually robust and challenging training - informed by and contributing to research - is likely to give future teachers the confidence and understanding they will need for their futures in an exposed and rarely uncontroversial profession.

The area where NQTs nationally feel least well satisfied with the preparation given them in their training is teaching in multicultural settings. Only one-third of NQTs consider their training was good or very good in preparing them to teach pupils from minority ethnic backgrounds and only about a quarter feel well or very well prepared to work with children whose English is an additional language. Part of the challenge for Sheffield Hallam University has been that it has recruited below its target of minority ethnic trainees. Securing better representation of minority ethnic students would promote wider acculturation. The School of Education and the new Faculty have pursued initiatives with the TTA to improve recruitment. But improving minority representation among trainees is only part of the challenge. The complexities and range of the issues faced by NQTs in multicultural settings are surely aspects of teaching practice which should form another component of a structured, incremental approach to in-service development in the first four or five years of NQTs' careers.

What constitutes appropriate teacher training has been subject to periodic and radical review. The College started when the majority of teachers had no certification at all. The 1950s and 1960s saw the the extension of the Certificate route from two years to three and then the addition of a further year for the BEd degree. The subsequent commitment to make teaching an all-graduate profession was fulfilled largely by concentrating the bulk of training nationally on the PGCE, a trend clear by 1980.

The 1990s saw increased government pressure to realign training to practitioner development within schools. Opinion within teacher education remains sceptical about the transformative potential of such a realignment. Given also the increased expectations placed upon ITT, it is easy to see why the expansion of ITT provision in the 1990s did not herald a new dawn for ITT providers.

Perhaps there is an increasing recognition that teachers, like medical doctors and lawyers, should not be regarded as fully-fledged, autonomous practitioners as soon as they complete their induction year following basic professional training. One way to prepare for a more sequential structure for professional development is to provide master's level modules within the PGCE, which can then be counted for credit towards a master's degree studied part-time during, say, the first four or five years of teaching. Such an approach to the PGCE modules is currently under discussion within Education. It could build on close collaborative work in CPD which has long been undertaken with local authorites. It also offers the opportunity of working with the TDA's stategy on integrated staff development. It might even create ways of lessening the sheer overload of skills and aptitudes that trainees in ITT are expected to acquire and reduce the immediate pressure on highly-motivated NQTs to perform well in aspects of the profession where they feel, nationally, their preparation has not been strong.

Southbourne
37 Clarkehouse Road

The oldest house on the campus lies at the northern edge on Clarkehouse Road, on land which had been leased from the Broomhall Park Estate. In 1819 Charles Brookfield (1772-1851) built a large stucco villa called Southbourne. Brookfield was a solicitor with Brookfield & Gould in Paradise Square, a firm which had been founded in 1787 by his uncle John Brookfield, prosecutor of James Montgomery (poet and founder of the Sheffield Iris, imprisoned in 1795 for outspoken articles).

Early photographs show the house little different from today, with the exception of a fine conservatory on the west end. It was a seven bedroom house with three dressing rooms, and included stabling for six horses and a peach house.

Southbourne as a residential property in the 1800s

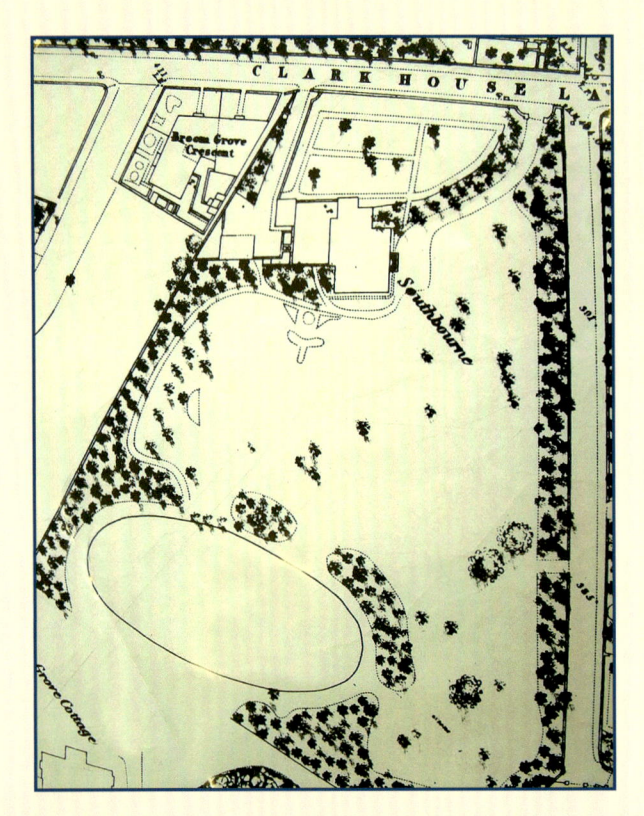

In the 1850s, Southbourne became the home of Abram Brooksbank, manufacturer of files, saws and table cutlery at Malinda Works, 25 Malinda Street; his initials appear in stained glass in the porch. He was mayor of Sheffield in 1880.

On his death the house was bought by Alderman Joseph Gamble, steel manufacturer of Moss & Gamble Bros. at Western Works in Rockingham Street. An active local politician, he was a councillor from 1871, alderman from 1890 and mayor in 1891. His reputation says it all, *'…it may be said 'It's dogged as does it… he has been a hard worker all his life… his speeches are not models of literary elegance'* (Notes and Queries, Sept 1900). But he was also a Ruskinian expert and active in opening up the countryside.

Map of Southbourne, 1853

On Gamble's death in 1907 the College bought Southbourne with three acres for £4,000, and put in plans to add wings to accommodate 60 men, the Principal and family, domestic staff and a dining hall for 120 students, at a cost of over £19,000. The new building is described as *'quite convincing Neo-Regency with broad eaves and bowed bays'* (Harman & Minnis 2004). In October 1911 it opened as a residence, the location proving very suitable to keep the men and women as far apart as possible, since the women students lived at Collegiate Hall!

In the grounds, a large oval pond which pre-dated the house (either ornamental or part of the water supply) was filled in but not without problems - in November 1909 a neighbour had to be compensated as he drew water from it. The line of the pond is still visible today in the shrubs around the tennis courts.

The two new Southbourne wings were named Park and Grove (Bottom and Top), and the Crescent magazine records fierce competition between them - a world of corridor concerts and initiation ceremonies, *'Bottom Grove evangelist choir were a disturbing influence on would-be workers above'*… *'Top Grove Wash House Male Voice Choir and Park's unquenchable Irish tenor.'*

Alderman J Gamble, Sheffield Weekly News, Notes and Queries, 1900

'Let Southbourne Common Room ever be the meeting-place of all the men, the palace of ping-pong, solo, chess and jazz. 'Keep your feet off the furniture' and 'Put your paper back in the rack' but go on enjoying the comradeship this room offers.' (Crescent 1938). In the 1950s concerts were held in the Common Room on Sunday evenings to raise funds for a student TB sanatorium. New armchairs arrived *'not correctly designed for sleeping in!'* Certain windows of Bottom Grove were left unlocked for late entry.

Southbourne in the 1940s

Southbourne
37 Clarkehouse Road

The Principals lived in the old house and acted as wardens. Pearson practised golf in the grounds and it became the home of the famous garden parties.

In 1935 HMIs reported that in Southbourne *'the stock of bed linen seems small and sheets are only changed fortnightly!'* In World War Two the view from the buildings made them very suitable for firewatching, and the students helped put out many fires in the area. The buildings were refurbished in the early 1960s into double rooms, and then in 1988 the buildings were converted to teaching accommodation, the shared rooms being no longer popular.

Group of men students outside Southbourne in the 1940s

Southbourne today

Parkholme
30 Collegiate Crescent

The Broomhall Park Estate had been bought as an investment by a solicitor, James Watson of Shirecliffe Hall, and used as farmland until the time was right for development; he then started leasing plots to speculative builders. The first house built was Parkholme in 1842, for William Hutchinson, a prosperous cutler. It was a plain Georgian style house with Doric pillars supporting the pedimented front porch.

Between around 1900 and 1930, it was occupied by Seth Whiteley, principal of Whiteley's Business College (a secretarial school) at 37 Surrey Street. From around 1930 to 1959, Major George Barnsley, owner of the Cornish Works and maker of files and rasps, was in residence.

Map of Parkholme, 1890

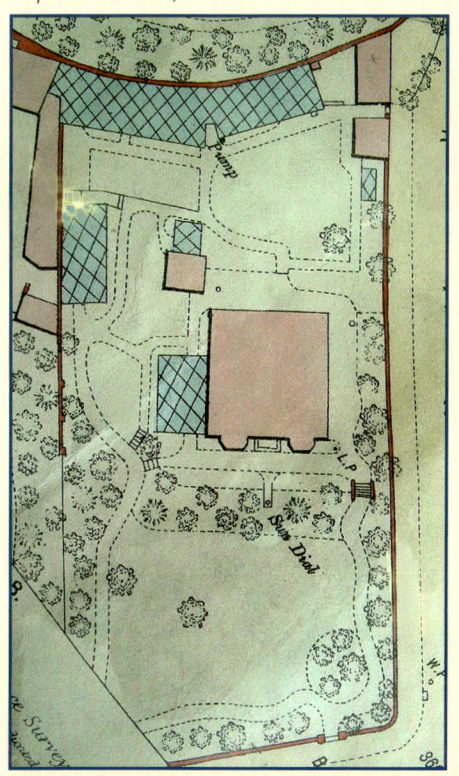

Parkholme was purchased by the College and opened as lodgings for 17 men in 1959. Phyllis and Jessie looked after the residents.

In 1960 women were lodging in Parkholme, but it was then converted to teaching accommodation; by 1968 it was the English department and later became a professional centre for geography education into the 1990s.

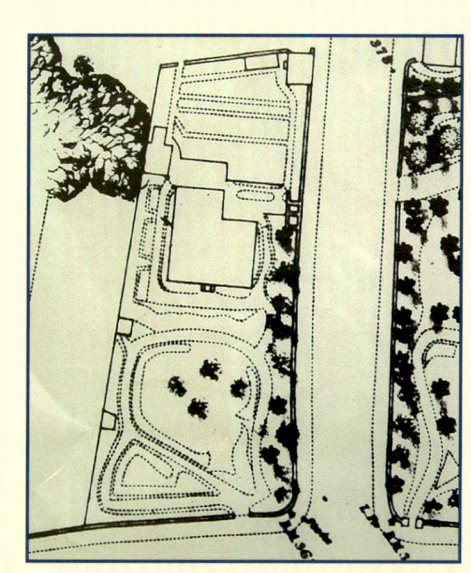

Map of Parkholme, 1853

Oaklands
46 Collegiate Crescent

Oaklands was built in 1849 by William Burgoyne Fennell, a solicitor at 3 Vicar Lane, and his wife Charlotte; they also acquired the plot to the north which became a pleasure garden. The fact that it was not developed left the way clear to build Marshall Hall in 1960. The Fennells occupied the house until 1879 when it was sold to Sir William Leng (1825-1902), founder and editor of the Sheffield Telegraph, who lived there until his death in 1902 - see the item about Leng.

The auction sale plans from 1902 give a good impression of the house, with its pleasure garden to the north (including kitchen garden, tennis lawn, gardener's house, three-horse stable), coach house and long greenhouse with vinery to the side of the house. A large conservatory on the south-east corner can still be traced today, and the fine plasterwork and carved staircase in the hall have survived. The front door on the east side of the house opened into morning and drawing rooms, with study and kitchen behind, and range of cellars below. The large room with two bay windows on the south-west corner was the dining room. Butler's pantry and servants' hall occupied the north-west corner. Upstairs on the first floor were five bedrooms and a billiard room, with a further three bedrooms and linen store on the second floor. One of these second floor bedrooms had fine balconies. There were bathrooms and a WC on both floors and the plans record that *'the Sanitary System was constructed recently at considerable expenditure,… and is believed to be in first class order'*.

Having increased its student numbers, the College bought the house in 1930 for £3,100, to house 30 men. It was threatened with closure when numbers were cut again in 1936. Strong memories survive of

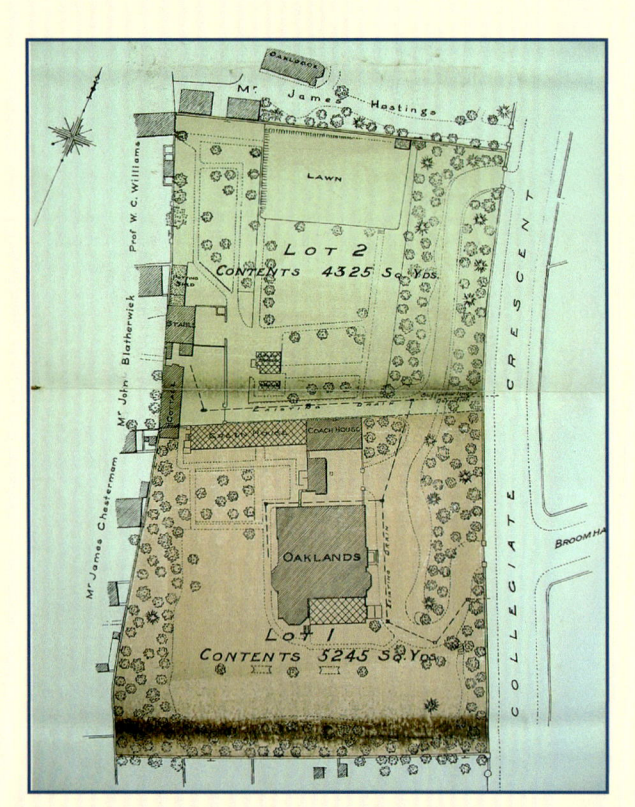

Oaklands around 1900

Oaklands sale plan, 1902

living in Oaklands - of the billiard table, 1940s resident warden Mr Sussams and his family; *'none of us will ever forget Oaklands, however hard some of us may try… the sick room, Rio, the cellar, Smutty'* (Crescent 1937). The students appreciated the new hall and gym nearby - *'for the improvements at College we have nothing but praise'* (Crescent 1938) and noted that *'study hours are enlivened by… the happy smiling faces of the College maidens during Country Dancing!'*

During and after World War Two, it was variously occupied by university students and by women. In the 1950s it became the main administrative centre, housing the Senior Common Room, Registrar and three staff including finance on the ground floor, and the principal and deputy principal's offices on the first floor. It was then threatened both with extension and demolition, before being converted to teaching space when the College management offices moved to College House in the early 1970s.

Oaklands today

Oaklands
46 Collegiate Crescent

Staff and male student group, Oaklands, 1945-46

Staff and female student group, Oaklands, 1944-45

Collegiate Hall
Ecclesall Road

The imposing building of Collegiate Hall provided residential accommodation for women students at the College for about 60 years. It began with the Collegiate School former headmaster's house at the centre, built in 1837, which provided a home for the first Lady Superintendent (later Deputy Principal) - Mrs Henry was *'the great Lady of Collegiate Hall'* (Crescent 1947) - and 27 women.

In August 1905 tenders were approved, and detailed plans drawn up for the west wing of Collegiate Hall; the walls were to be built of 'Crookes rockies'.

Former heads' house at the centre of Collegiate Hall

The west wing opened in 1906. This was followed in 1910 by the almost identical east wing, to house a total of 150 women (for more detail, see item on Accommodation). Each wing cost about £10,000 to build.

The housekeeper and maids lived at the back of the central former head's house, where the kitchen and larder were located. The first floor of the old house became the sick bay.

During World War One, the new furnishings were ripped out to turn the building into a hospital with 400 beds for wounded soldiers (see item on World War One), and the College students moved back in 1919.

Mrs Lysbeth Henry, first Lady Superintendent

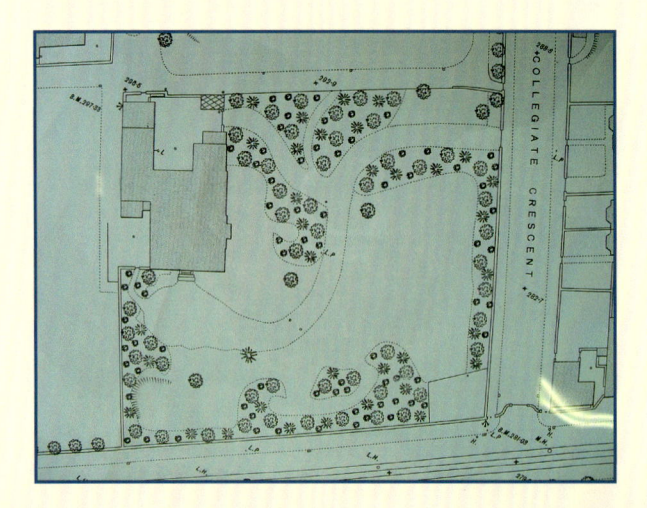

There then followed a long period of stability. Collegiate Hall was described in 1941 (Crescent) as a *'tall venerable grey-stoned ivy-covered building... Gaunt fire escapes standing like sentinels on each side... here through the portal we enter a long stone corridor, dim and unimposing... at each end... we observe stone stairways ascending to the unknown...'*

Plan of Old Head's House, 1904

Collegiate Hall sitting room

Collegiate Hall sitting room

Architects Gibbs & Flockton plan, 1905

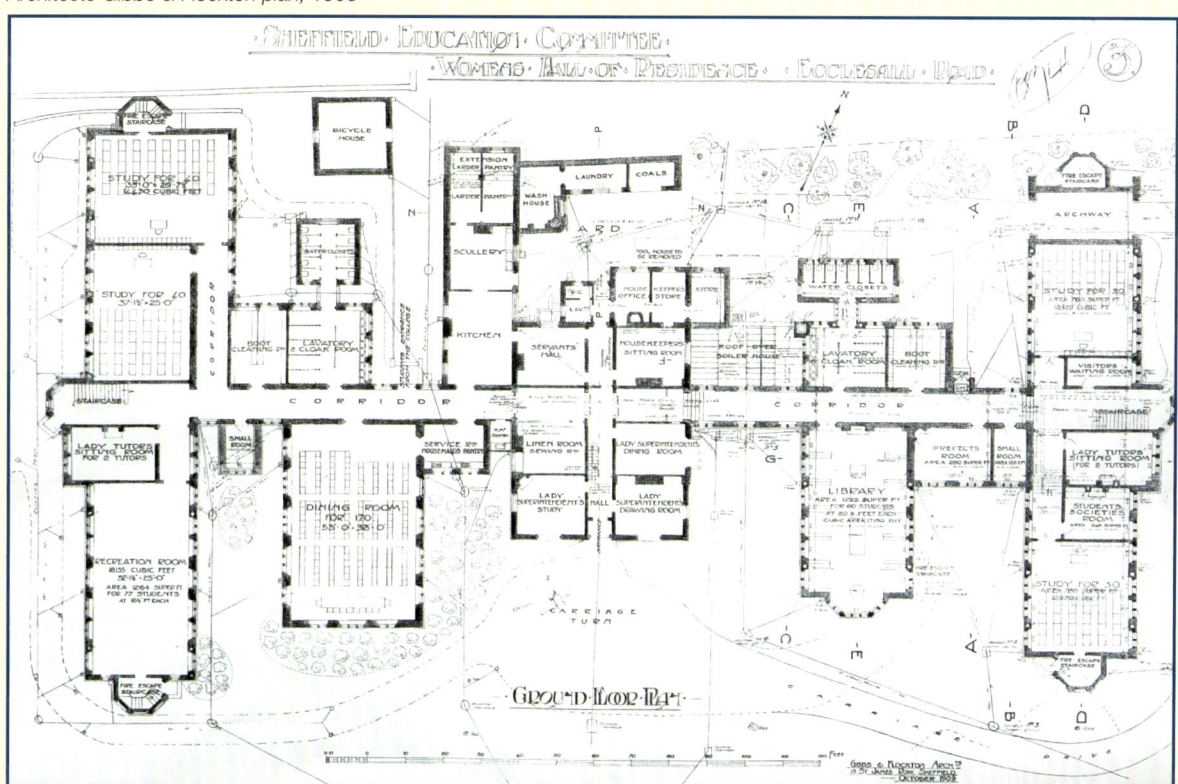

Collegiate Hall

Collegiate Hall remained a residence up to the early 1960s, sometimes latterly for men, until the new halls were built. The College managers had contemplated converting the cubicles into small rooms but it would have proved expensive, and it was felt that the stone building with rooms larger than were usually allowed was suited to academic use. It was converted to teaching space for science and mathematics in the west wing and geography, art, craft, French and music in the east wing. An animal house was built at the west end in the 1970s, and a single storey extension on the back (now Saunders) housed woodworking and metalworking shops.

Saunders today

Collegiate Hall today

Woodworking in the 1960s

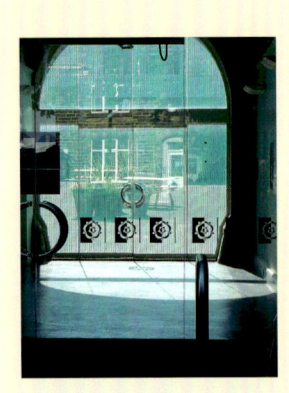

The Animal House

Collegiate Hall was totally refurbished again in 2001, to establish sports science laboratories and other specialized teaching and professional space, and provides a fine landmark building for the campus.

College House, formerly Oakdale
36 Collegiate Crescent

College House, formerly known as Oakdale, was one of the early houses built on the Broomhall Park Estate, on land leased in 1852. It is plain in style compared to 34 and 38 Collegiate Crescent; the cornices are plain and there are few stone carvings.

In the early 1860s it was occupied by Baron James Wehli, a professional musician who played in royal circles and set up an orchestra in Sheffield, and his wife. Wehli gave piano lessons to wealthy families; there were five pianos in the house, listed in an inventory dated 1866.

In the 1870-1880s it was occupied by John Edward Barker, barrister at 42 Bank Street, and c1902-27 by Henry Barlow Sandford, solicitor at 30 Bank Street, who had been a pupil at the Collegiate School. He was Conservative councillor for Ecclesall in 1904.

By the 1950s the house had become too big for a private home and became offices for Phillips Furnishing Stores, Kennings Ltd motor car agents, and meat dealers Fatstock Marketing Co.; there was a safe in the cellars, later used as secure storage for exam papers!

In 1970 the property was bought by the College for £30,000 to use as an administrative centre: board room, principal's and senior staff offices, admissions tutor and student records in the attic. In 1976 it was occupied for three weeks during a student protest over cuts and job shortages. Later the building housed the Education Management centre until reverting back to administrative offices.

Shelving in College House cellar

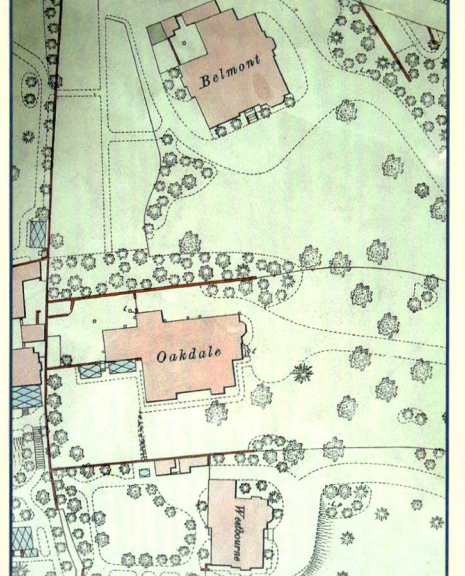

Student occupation in 1976

Map of College House, 1890

Broomgrove Road houses

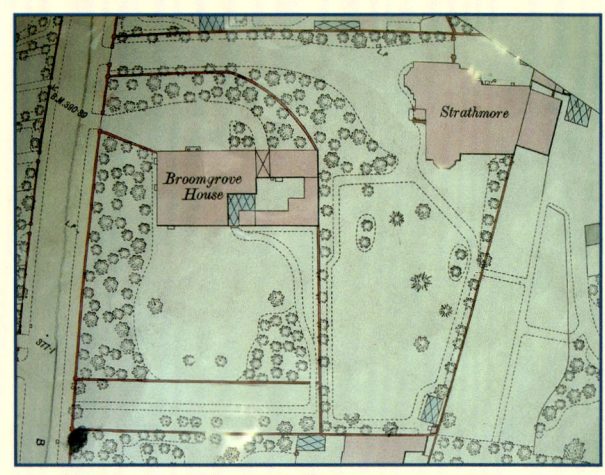

The western edge of Collegiate Campus follows Broomgrove Road. This land, still with a clear boundary wall down the middle of the campus, was previously part of the Broomhall Park Estate, owned by the Spooner family. Its development was less planned than the east side of the campus owned by Watson.

The earliest development was a farm called Brooms Grove, replaced by two Victorian houses, Nos. 9 and 11, which occupied the site of the present Broomgrove Hall of Residence.

The earliest known owner of Brooms Grove was William Spooner, already in residence at the time of his marriage in 1795; the house appears on Fairbanks' map of 1795 with L-shaped outbuildings to the north-west and orchard or garden to the east, down a short lane from Clarkehouse Road. It was sold on his death in 1831 to Samuel Parker (1791-c1871), bone and horn merchant with premises at canal-side Parkers Wharf. Samuel moved from Broomhill, demolishing the older house and building slightly to the south-east. A second house (called Strathmore on the 1890 map) was built at the back of the plot, probably for his son. Parker may also have constructed the new north-south Broomgrove Road.

Map of Broomgrove House, 1890

The houses were occupied by the Auxiliary Territorial Service during World War Two, and were bought by the College in the late 1940s by compulsory purchase order for £3,500, as residence for about 40 men, who used the Southbourne dining and common rooms. *'At 22.30 hours on the 10th September 1951, the newly posted hand-picked members of No. 9 Battalion Broomgrove Light Infantry paraded for the first time…'* The attic of No. 11 became an observatory, because it was the bedroom of the president of the Astronomical Society! (Crescent 1952) The houses were demolished to build the Hall which opened in 1962 for 160 men.

Nos.13 and 17 Broomgrove Road are owned by architects Hadfield, Cawkwell & Davidson.

Another early house was The Grove, No. 23, a fine house leased from 1853; it was occupied in the late Nineteenth-century by Henry Searl, of Sybry, Searls & Co, Cannon St Works on Carlisle Street, manufacturers of cast, shear, blister and spring steel.

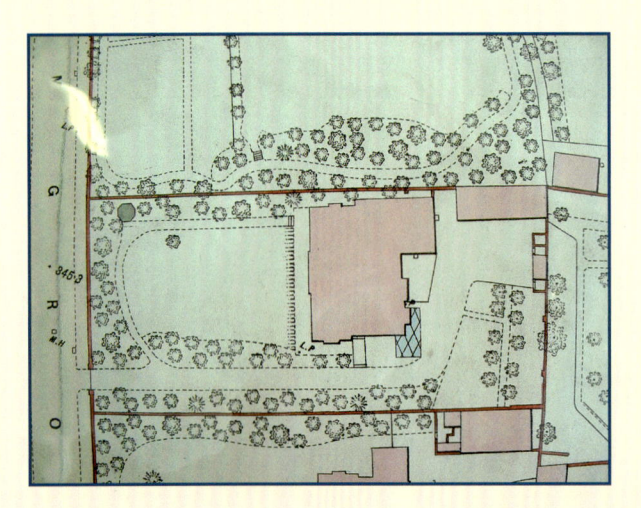

Map of 23 Broomgrove Road, 1890

Between around 1900 and 1960, it was lived in by a series of professors, directors and solicitors, until it became an orphanage for the city's Childrens' Department in the 1960s. The house was bought by the College in 1974 for £15,000, for use as a student hostel; today it is the University nursery.

25 Broomgrove Road was built around 1860 and occupied in the last few decades of the Nineteenth-century by John Blatherwick, sugar broker and fruit merchant at 45 Exchange Street. Its demolition was recommended in 1971 to make way for communal facilities; it was purchased in 1972 by the College, and fortunately retained for use as a staff club, though again threatened by plans in the early 1990s, and has been the Mathematics Education Centre for many years.

Further down the east side of the road, the plots grew gradually smaller and were developed later. Nos. 27-41 were built around 1870 and occupied by a succession of professional and trades people. Nos. 27-31 were purchased by the College in the late 1960s. In 1969 a brewery had offered money towards a lounge and bar at 27 Broomgrove Road, and No. 29 was the Deputy Principal's home after it was a men's residence; they were demolished in 1971 to make way for the new Pearson Sports Hall.

23 Broomgrove Road

25 Broomgrove Road

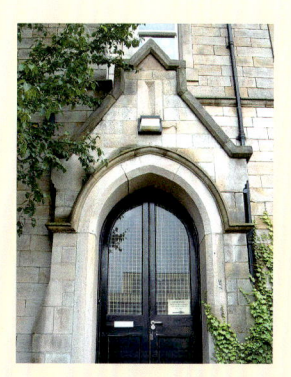

Broomgrove Road houses

The remaining houses were the subject of intense scrutiny in the early 1970s during the period of rapid expansion and reorganisation. No. 35 was being used as tutorial space in 1974. No. 37 was bought by the College in 1969 for £5,500 to be the Deputy Principal's home. In 1974 the College gained approval to purchase No. 39 for £12,000.

Nos. 43-57 were built around 1880. No. 45 was acquired at auction for £11,250 in 1974. No. 47 was rented by the College in 1906 as a hostel for women while Collegiate Hall was being built, but never belonged to the College. No. 49 was bought by the College in 1965 for £2,350 for residential use; it housed 11 men in the late 1960s, and was later used for tutorials.

35 Broomgrove Road

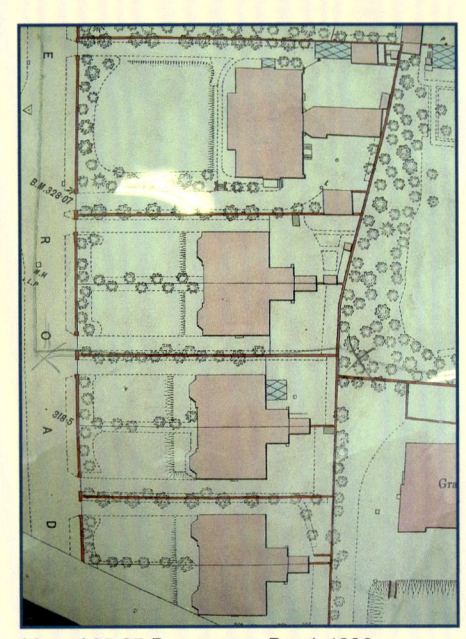

Map of 25-37 Broomgrove Road, 1890

No. 51 was bought in the 1970s and has always been used for tutorial and office space. No. 53 was purchased in 1973 for £18,000, built on land which was leasehold for 800 years from 1881, at £9 per year. It had been occupied by cutlery manufacturer Edmund Priestman in 1902, and cabinetmaker Myer Cantor in 1927. It was later used for tutorial and office space, as it still is today, linked with No. 51.

No. 55 was bought by the College in 1965 for £3,000 as a residence for nine men.

No. 57 Broomgrove Road was acquired in the late 1990s and 41 Broomgrove Road was eventually bought at auction in 1994 although never used.

In 1972 compulsory purchase orders were submitted for 39, 41 and 45 Broomgrove Road with a proposal for a new library; CPOs were already in hand for 47, 53 and 57, with plans for new science and art blocks. There was a public enquiry in September 1972, but the College was not successful and was forced to build the library on the tennis courts.

All the buildings in current university ownership are now used for staff offices and small teaching rooms. Some houses have been sold by Sheffield Hallam University back into the private sector; Nos. 41, 47, 55 and 57 Broomgrove Road are currently in private ownership, and have ensured the survival of the row of houses.

43 Broomgrove Road

Mundella, formerly Belmont
34 Collegiate Crescent

One of the few houses on the Broomhall Park Estate appearing on the 1851 map, Belmont was first occupied in the 1850s by William White, publisher of the trade directories. The house is on leasehold land for 800 years from Sept 1852 at £29 per year.

Soon after it was built, it became the residence of the Vicars of Sheffield, the first to live there being The Reverend Dr Thomas Sale, who also had an official residence at 5 St James Row. From then on, it was occupied by the following Vicars: Rowley Hill (from 1873), Archdeacon Blakeney (1877), and Archdeacon John Rashdall Eyre (1895) who was a classical scholar and champion hammer thrower! In the 1901 census he was living there with five children and four servants. From 1912 it was occupied by Herbert Gresford Jones, followed by Carr (1920), John Darbyshire (1922) and the Bishop of Sheffield Alfred Jarvis (1931).

The house was named Belmont on 1905 and 1913 maps, but called Cathedral Vicarage on a 1935 map. It was renamed Mundella after the Sheffield educationalist Anthony John Mundella (1825-97), Liberal MP for Sheffield in 1868-97, and an early advocate of compulsory education.

John Rashdall Eyre

In the 1950s and 1960s, this house and Montgomery next door were occupied by the United Coke and Chemicals Co Ltd (later British Steel Corporation) as staff training hostels. They built the squash courts between the two houses. The house was bought by the Education Authority for the College in 1972 and initially used as a residence for the year four BEd students with Senior Tutor Constance Gilbey as warden. Subsequently it became teaching and office space. It still retains many original features - fine plaster cornices, a staircase with twisted metal spindles and unusual ornate barge boards, thought to be moulded plaster and horse hair.

Main Building
See also Collegiate School

The 1836 school building designed by Weightman consisted of a central hall with large windows flanked by canopied niches and two classrooms at each side; it cost £10,000 to build. Behind it was a fives court. In 1885 when the grammar school moved in, a wing was added at the west end of the building. In 1906 soon after the opening of the College, a two storey block was added at the east end of Main Building, designed by Gibbs & Flockton, to provide additional classroom accommodation.

As the College settled down, more science laboratory and classroom space was planned, to enable it to be independent of the University of Sheffield. City Architect F.E.P. Edwards was commissioned to bring the façade of Main Hall forward by 14 feet and add buttresses, raise the central hall to two storeys and add a continuous upper storey for laboratories, gym or examination room, and other rooms, while retaining the general proportions and detail of the original building on the exterior. This was a major feat. The Collegiate School hall later became the College assembly hall/gym and library. The original hand-painted plans survive, showing on the west side at ground floor level four classrooms (for geography, English and mathematics) and the lady tutor's room, and at first floor level a classroom for art and nature study lab; on the east side there was a science lab and men's common room (later used for needlework and handicraft) upstairs, with a common room, cloakrooms and principal's office below.

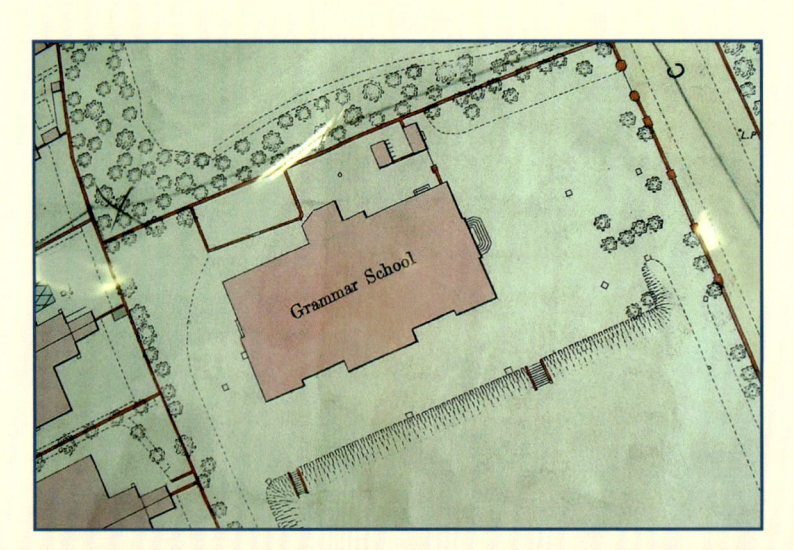

Map of Main Building, 1890

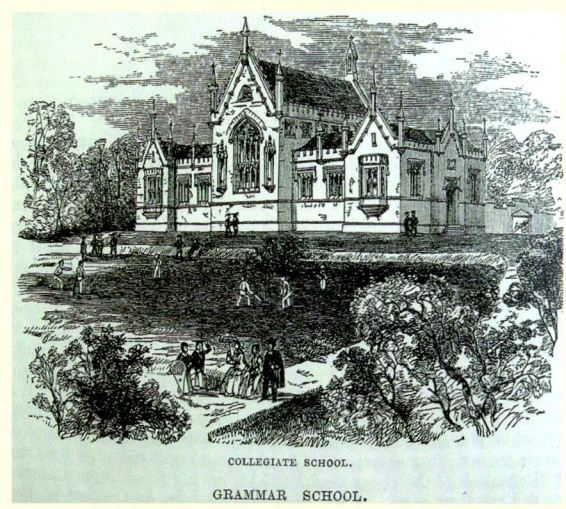

Original Collegiate School building, 1836

Main Building in use as the Grammar School in the 1880s with new west wing

Main Building in 1906 with new east wing

Two storey Main Building, opened in 1911

Main Building
See also Collegiate School

Original Gibbs & Flockton drawings, 1905

Staff and student group photo, 1905

111

Main Building
See also Collegiate School

The opening ceremony on 18 October 1911 for the new two storey building and new wings at Collegiate Hall was attended by the Lord Chancellor, Lord Loreburn. The students sang him the College song written by The Reverend Pearson and Dr Coward, and he reminded the gathering of the transcendent importance of *'the spirit in which men approach their work, the self-restraint, self control, self reliance, the moral courage, the wish to help others and the recognition that it is our duty to help other people as well as ourselves'*.

Lady Mayoress presenting medal during World War One

During World War One the building was part of the 3rd Northern Base Hospital - while refurbishing it in 2005, builders found travel warrents dated 1916, bibles and slippers beneath floorboards and walls.

Plans were drawn up for an art room to be added on the north-west first floor corner of Main Building in 1920. This brought the building up to almost 12,000 square feet of teaching and office space. During World War Two, teaching carried on almost as normal.

Inspectors criticised gym facilities in 1935, which led to a new building behind, housing assembly hall/theatre and gym which opened in 1938.

Following the 1955 HMI Inspection, it became clear that more small tutorial rooms and a central common room (which at that time was the large education room in Main Building where *'light refreshments beloved of all students'* were available) were urgently needed. In the early 1960s, when some of the teaching was moved to other buildings, the three libraries (lending, reference and teaching practice) were brought together (see item on Libraries), and remained in Main Building until the new library was built in 1976. The senior staff moved out to use Oaklands as the administrative centre. Main Building at that time also housed professional studies, psychology and a resource centre.

In the early 1970s, still planning for additional numbers, Main Building was considered to be *'neither attractive nor convenient'* and *'antiquated'*. The Governing Body Buildings Committee agreed in principle that *'on the grounds of economy and utility the building*

Students and staff, seated left to right Miss Ashton, Miss Bowker and Miss Brooke, 1945

should be demolished' (March 1973) and replaced with a fine new four storey building; this was never implemented! Instead it was agreed to convert the library into a senior common room and coffee lounge.

The building has remained teaching space and has on the face of it changed little over the century. In 2005 a complete renovation was undertaken; the entire building was made watertight and a new toilet block and staircase were added. All teaching rooms are now equipped to the standards of the best seminar and lecture rooms in the University.

Main Building with temporary huts used for teaching, 1967

Lino cut from Crescent magazine

Main Building today

Sheffield Hallam University's commitment to providing a modern learning environment

Recent trends

At its centenary, Education at Sheffield Hallam University remained a major national contributor to teacher training. The number of Initial Teacher Training students contracted by the Training and Development Agency makes Sheffield Hallam University the seventh largest provider in England. For 2005-2006 it was allocated 888 new entrants, plus 62 new places for the separate Graduate Teacher Programme organised through the Yorkshire and Derbyshire Training Partnership. Taking into account the students on two-year and three-year programmes, the total number of trainees has returned to the earlier highs reached in the late 1960s and early 1970s. The relative commitment of Sheffield Hallam University and the University of Sheffield to Initial Teacher Training is striking; the total number of allocated funded places is 1,453 for Sheffield Hallam University and 153 for the University of Sheffield.

These overall numbers, however, hide a number of major shifts. About half the students are enrolled in secondary ITT; 50 years ago the focus was essentially on primary. Over two-thirds of all those entering ITT programmes each year take the PGCE and only one-third take the three-year or, for some, two-year undergraduate courses. That massive shift to postgraduate training marks a radical change of emphasis from the 1970s. And 70 per cent of the entering PGCE students take secondary routes. Their qualifications at entry are rising, with one-third of the secondary one-year PGCE trainees having a 2:1 or better in 1999 while over half did so by 2003.

Another vital characteristic of the provision is the focus on priority or shortage subjects at the secondary level. This is a major commitment to meeting national needs in particular secondary specialisms. The TTA/TDA has, over many years, identified seven priority subjects in secondary ITT and Sheffield Hallam University provides training in six of them. Moreover, in four of those Sheffield Hallam University is among the largest national providers.

Commitment to shortage subjects raises its own challenges. There are periodic difficulties in recruiting to the target numbers provided. For example, if PGCE mathematics nationally depended on recruiting new graduates, it would fail to meet its targets because there are simply not enough new graduates each year in mathematics to meet the national demand for new mathematics teacher trainees. And in some subjects it is difficult to find additional school placements of the quality required. Sustaining good quality placements is important because Ofsted reports consistently find good provision and rigorous standards across the secondary programmes. Placements in schools are not always as readily available as they would be if the University had fewer trainees or directed its efforts to other subjects. On the other hand, important research, consultancy and project work has been undertaken by academics from the shortage subjects, most extensively in mathematics and science, and their pedagogic commitment to teacher education has been strong.

Historically, teacher training at Sheffield City College promoted mature student access. Specific programmes for mature students were still unusual enough to attract press attention in the early 1970s. But the national picture is now one in which teaching is seen by many as an attractive second or postponed career. Over half the trainees in secondary are nowadays aged 25 years or over when they begin their training. Yet for many mature returners the option of a full-time, year-long course for a PGCE is impractical or unattractive. During the 1990s, the TTA responded to non-traditional students' needs - and to the need to recruit non-traditional trainees - with various initiatives which Sheffield Hallam University was quick to join. A part-time PGCE was introduced in primary. A more challenging initiative to deliver has been the flexible or modular PGCE, typically involving distributed and distance learning. This is offered both in primary and six secondary subjects. The level of demand is indicated by the provision for 130 new entrants in 2005-2006. A further route was developed by the TTA in the early 2000s. This Graduate Teacher Programme allows for graduates to seek and secure teaching assistant posts in schools and then, jointly with the schools, to work in schools and train for Qualified Teacher Status at the same time. The University took the lead in establishing the Yorkshire and Derbyshire Training Partnership and this collaborative venture has been well reviewed by Ofsted. Numbers for the GTP have grown steadily since it started in 2002-2003. The University has an outstanding record for implementing new training initiatives to provide intending teachers with the choice of routes suited to their preferences and needs.

Secondary ITT numbers allocated for 2005-2006 by TDA

	Sheffield Hallam University number of new entrants	Notable national rank in number allocated
Priority subjects		
Design and technology including engineering	102	1
Science	100	4
Mathematics	90	3
ICT	60	
Modern languages	30	
Religious education	20	
Other secondary		
Business studies	53	2=
English	31	
Physical education	26	
Citizenship	15	
Vocational secondary		
Applied ICT	20	
Engineering	8	new in 2005

As a result of this commitment, the provision of ITT has become very complex. The TTA/TDA distributes student numbers by region and by institution, both modified by Ofsted quality ratings, and places trainees in each subject discipline widely across the country. Under TTA/TDA policies, it is difficult for providers to build up large cohorts in all the subjects they offer. There is also the practical impediment to doing that created by the need to find schools within a reasonable distance where the trainees can undertake their teaching practice. In primary there are six different programmes by specialist age-group, by undergraduate, three-year, or postgraduate route, or by full-time, part-time, or flexible/modular mode. In secondary there are twelve subjects (with some overlap in two) at PGCE. Three of those are also taught at two-year and three-year undergraduate levels, and six of them are available in flexible/modular mode at PGCE level.

The curriculum varies according to route. Opportunities exist within this varied provision to seek common elements in methodology and pedagogy. Most modules in the primary undergraduate and PGCE programmes are shared by all students. On the other hand, the PGCE secondary curriculum provides one core module, General Professional Studies, though heavily weighted in the syllabus, and a range of subject modules, typically focused on teaching and learning, planning and organisation, research methods and subject knowledge enhancement in the individual subjects. The shift from the late 1980s to increased time on school practice means that students spend only 12 of the 36 week PGCE programme taking courses in the University, which amounts to less than a semester, while the bulk of their programme is on placement. Students taking the undergraduate programme spend 120 days, equivalent to 24 weeks, on teaching practice. In the 1960s students spent half that amount of time in schools.

The sheer number and range of placements has led to the establishment of a partnership office and to a concerted drive to improve relationships with partner schools and ensure the consistency of students' experience on placements. On the whole, schools cannot take more than a small number of trainees on placements. In 2002-2003, for example, 30 of the partner secondary schools/colleges took only one trainee each, and 31 took two or three trainees. At the other end of the scale, only six partners took 10 to 12 trainees and only four took over 12. In all, out of 129 partners involved in training secondary teachers, 100 took six or fewer trainees. Ensuring that such an extensive partnership works well - and there were also over 600 primary partner schools in the system - requires far more extensive administration than it did 30 years ago. One critical point made about two secondary subjects by Ofsted inspections in the late 1990s concerned the training of school mentors and their proactive involvement in turn with student training. A variety of initiatives, in part funded by the TTA, have assisted in strengthening the links between the University and the partner schools. Links made by individual tutors and the mentoring provided by them remain central to the effective working of this wide range of partnerships. It is not unusual for academics to make 30-50 extended external visits a year, with obvious consequences for time commitments and time available for other teaching preparation.

In common with colleagues in other Schools of the University, academic staff in the School of Education reported in 2000 that an aspect of their job which provided outstandingly high satisfaction was the stimulation of working with students. The daily process of preparing for, engaging in and developing practice is a major and fulfilling part of the work of teacher education. This process occurs within the context of rapidly changing technology in education. Ofsted in 2000 reported for secondary that access and use of ICT was typically good and that teaching resources were good or very good across the subjects. But a continuing challenge is the amount of time available for re-thinking and then re-working teaching strategies in the light of rapid technological advances.

Many academics and trainees are strongly motivated to make a difference to the aspirations and lives of school students in a region of continuing educational under-achievement. Four of the local authorities with which Education works most closely are Barnsley, Doncaster, Rotherham and Sheffield. They are among the 50 most economically deprived in England, with the region's poverty worsening in relation to national norms since 1991. One third of Sheffield's population live in wards which are among the 10 per cent most deprived wards in the country. This economic deprivation resulted in out-migration and population decline, by 1.7 per cent, in 1991-2001, in sharp contrast to England and Wales's increase in population by 2.5 per cent overall. The impact of economic deprivation on educational attainment is striking. In 2000, Sheffield came 138 out of 150 English LEAs in the percentage of 18-19 year olds accepted into higher education. In 2001 at 15 plus years, the percentages of students achieving five A* - C grades at GCSE were

Barnsley	35.1	Sheffield	41.9
Doncaster	39.9	Rotherham	43

These results compared unfavourably with the national average of 50 per cent. Even though significant increases in the proportion of students achieving this range of grades occurred between 1998 and 2001 - especially in Barnsley - the national level also rose, meaning that a considerable gap remained. In 2004 the evaluation of primary schools' results placed Sheffield's 115 primary schools as a group 129th out of 149 English Education Authorities. Individually 59 of those 115 primary schools - over half - produced scores below the national average.

Part of the stimulus and challenge many find in teacher education and in training for teaching is the concerted effort to overcome this pattern of under-achievement. Building upon the individual sense of determination displayed by so many teachers - including Sheffield Hallam University trainees - there has been a raft of initiatives. The most ambitious in trying to secure a step-change in Sheffield has been the programme to rebuild schools or extensively renew their fabric, in order to provide a more positive, healthy and usable environment for learning and teaching. The other step-change project in the region is the South Yorkshire e-Learning Project running from August 2003 to December 2006. This is a vast scheme, kick-started by £7 millions of EU funding and drawing together some £60 millions in total, to create a completely new online system for accessible learning and teaching materials. As far as new learning methods and resources are concerned, this project offers an impressive potential base for recreating the region's learning environment and for enhancing the sense of self-worth among learners and teachers that flows from access to and engagement with a positive learning environment.

There is a growing awareness at both national and local levels that, as many academics have long argued, more holistic approaches are needed to tackling problems of educational under-achievement and social and economic deprivation. Much expertise has been developed within Sheffield Hallam University in the analysis of urban renewal and community regeneration. In order to try to develop synergies across the academic portfolio, the University restructured its academic schools into four faculties in 2003-2004. The new organisational alignment, with Education becoming part of the Faculty of Development and Society, focuses planning and resources on exploiting potential for growth and offers opportunities for positioning Education for growth in its many activities which are not Initial Teaching Training. The fact that the TDA will cut trainee numbers nation-wide substantially in the next decade underscores the importance of further diversification. Consultancy and contract work, already well established in Education in the early 2000s, will have an increasingly significant role within the new Faculty.

Consultancy and contract work accounted for about 35 per cent of the School of Education's activities in 2003-2004 when it merged into the Faculty of Development and Society. The leading single area of contract work was undertaken by the Centre for Science Education with its long-established record of delivering projects to foster school students' interest in science. The work undertaken involved national initiatives and projects contracted with education authorities and education trusts throughout the UK. The second area was a growing volume of work in postgraduate CPD, often negotiated with LEAs or schools to provide diploma or master's degree enhancement in specific aspects of career development, especially in leadership and management. Finally, contract research grew in the 2000s. In 2002-2003, for example, some 32 bids were submitted and the nine successful ones generated £505,763 in income. They included evaluation work for the Qualification and Curriculum Authority, the South Yorkshire Learning and Skills Council, and Research Machines, in relation to its project management of the South Yorkshire e-Learning Project. Individual schemes where evaluation occurred included 'Pathways to Success', and the 'Leading from the Middle' Programme. One major project in the early 2000s was the local evaluation in the north and east of England of 'Crime Reduction in Secondary Schools' (CRISS) projects run by the Home Office. The evaluation involved 100 interviews with project staff, the analysis of 2,301 pupils' questionnaires, the observation of meetings, and in-depth interviews with pupils. As with the evaluation of LEA initiatives, the research thrust combines the analysis of statistical information and policy and project documents with the thorough use of interview and questionnaire responses to capture the practitioners' and students' perspectives in the round.

The role of research in Education is complex. The research base in the colleges was narrow and depended essentially on the individual preferences, motivations, and commitments of personal time made by lecturing staff. Some had strong scholarly interests and a few made distinctive scholarly contributions. But no research culture existed. Again, the Polytechnic allowed and often encouraged individuals to pursue their research interests. But no more concerted programme to foster research emerged until the late 1980s and early 1990s. Moreover, staff appointed were mainly engaged in Initial Teacher Training and nearly always came from teaching posts in schools, where they had neither the time nor the opportunity nor the need to engage in higher level research. Unlike many disciplines, education could not expect applicants for lectureships to have made substantial progress towards or completed a PhD at the time of appointment. Many academics, however, went on to undertake doctoral research. It is a considerable achievement that the research culture within the subject has been mainly home-grown. In 2001-2004, for example, four Education staff achieved personal chairs, with significant publications as at least a part of their contribution recognised by that designation.

But issues remain. Although Education has fostered research, the vast majority of Education staff do not publish on a significant or sustained scale. Only about 15 per cent of academics in Education itself were entered for the Reseach Assessment Exercise in 2001. The strategy for national research assessments in 1996 and 2001 was to group academics engaged in research in Education together, through the research leadership of the University's Learning and Teaching Research Institute. The Institute was established in 1994 as a central service, designed to conduct research and review pedagogic strategies and practices across the University as a whole. By 1996 these five research groups, which in 2001 had expanded to nine, involved academics from across the University. Since RAE 2001 the Institute has dropped the word Research from its title and has focussed more widely on pedagogic enhancement and inquiry. Some staff are permanently based in the Institute; others are seconded there for a semester or for substantially longer periods. The Institute has proved a fruitful catalyst for innovation and in drawing interested colleagues together to collaborate on a wide range of initiatives. This development as a central university service has provided another route by which Education staff can pursue their research interests and create new research collaborations.

The strategy for RAE submissions proved very frustrating. The outcome in 1996 was a reasonable 3a. In 2001 fewer staff were submitted but the outcome was the same. In fact, as the table shows, there was very little overall movement nationally into the adequately funded RAE grades - of four or higher - between 1996 and 2001. The total number of entries securing those higher grades increased by a mere three. And, indeed, the 3a grade went to only two more institutions in 2001 than the total of five years earlier. The impression of an overall enhancement to research outcomes in this unit of assessment arose largely because 21 institutions did not enter at all. Moreover, no 1992 university secured a four or five in 1996 and only one did so in 2001. Sheffield Hallam University's performance was very much in line with that of other major providers of Initial Teacher Training. The dilemma facing the University may be summarised simply. The overall challenge for the new university sector was to produce works of greater length embodying extensive original research. Much work at Sheffield Hallam University, however, was related to, and funded through, specific policy-driven or policy-related case studies, rather than to longer-term projects whose operation was made possible by research council grants.

During the period between RAE 1996 and RAE 2001, total research and research-related income attributed to the Education entry rose from £626,971 to £1,036,987. That increase resulted from cross-cutting trends. Research council funding fell, thus reducing opportunities for longer-term research programmes. Yet funding from UK central government bodies and from UK industry, commerce and public corporations rose, evidence of the growing drive for policy-driven research and the University's reputation for delivering it.

RAE results 1996 and 2001: Education unit of Assessment
Grades awarded and institutions receiving them

	1996	2001
Total Institutional entries	104	83
4 + 5 + 5*	30	33
3a	17	19
3b	20	22
1 + 2	37	9

In RAE 2001, research within the Education unit of assessment was focused on nine groups, four of which were most directly related to staff in Education. Those four represent continuing areas of research activity and development, in mathematics education, science education, policy and social issues in education and education management. The position of mathematics and science as long-term secondary shortage subjects, and the centrality of education management to any reform or improvement agenda, make these areas centrally important to some of the most challenging aspects of regional and national educational development. Policy and social issues in Education have involved aspects of school experience central to reform and relate critically to the agenda of the new Faculty of Development and Society.

In mathematics a central focus for research has been pedagogy, with particular attention given to the impact of ICT on subject teaching. Work has been done on competence in mathematics skills, adult learning in mathematics, and teachers' use of ICT for mathematics. Work on the use of multimedia and electronic resources in teaching led to the development of an international MSc in Multimedia Education and Consultancy; the leader of this project, Professor Brian Hudson, received a National Teaching Fellowship in 2004 in recognition of this work and to support its further development. Under the direction of Professor Bill Harrison (who was awarded an honorary doctorate by Sheffield Hallam University on his retirement in 2004) the Centre for Science Education built a leading national reputation, notable for its innovative approaches to engaging secondary school students with science. One major project in the late 1990s, the 'Pupil Research Initiative', funded by over £1 million across three years, was a major scheme for drawing practical, applied science into school work. Over many years the centre attracted a range of external funding from research councils, philanthropic trusts and major companies. Its standing was recognised in 2002-2003 when it joined a successful bid by the White Rose consortium of research-intensive universities - Leeds, Sheffield and York - to secure the new National Science Education Centre. The Centre is being constructed at York, while Sheffield Hallam University is the regional Science Education Centre for Yorkshire and the Humber, one of nine regional centres set up under this £50 million joint Wellcome Trust - DfES project.

Building on successful studies undertaken for LEAs, staff working on policy and social issues in Education have undertaken an increasing number of national consultancies. One, for example, concerned the involvement of parents in the choice of secondary schools for their children, with a major national project being completed for the DfEE and Office for National Statistics. Extensive work over many years has been undertaken on evaluating change agendas in schools. New areas of work have involved the national development of Higher Level Teaching Assistants. Within education management, the thrust of research has been school leadership, with an emphasis on schools as learning organisations, and the relationship of theory to education reform and managerialism in schools. Within the new Faculty much of the work in policy and social issues in education and education management have been drawn together in the Centre for Education Research established in 2004, with a total staff of nine. Among current or very recent projects are the

- Evaluation of the 'Leading from the Middle' programme for the National College of School Leadership
- Analysis of Pupils' Performance in science at Key Stage 3 for the Qualifications and Curriculum Authority
- Evaluation of Home School Agreements for DfES
- Investigation of the impact of e-learning on student learning outcomes in Further Education Colleges for the DfES
- Evaluation of SYeLP for Research Machines and the SYeLP partnership

In addition, the Centre's staff run a successful part-time EdD programme and manage the Yorkshire and Derbyshire Training Partnership. They also draw upon colleagues in other areas of Education, and more widely across the University, to provide effective multidisciplinary research teams, while at the same time fostering a wider research culture in Education.

Two reflections upon the role of research and the professional formation of teachers are in order. Nationwide participation in education affects over one quarter of the population at any one time. In 2001, about 16 million people in the UK were at school or in further and higher education as full-time or part-time students. Well over one million people were employed by schools, colleges and universities in teaching and supporting them. But from the research review of that year, the Higher Education Funding Council determined that there were only just under 650 academics in Education nation-wide who were doing research in departments judged to be attaining levels of international excellence in half and national levels of excellence in virtually all the rest of their research work. Moreover, 45 per cent of those academics were in university institutes and departments in central London and in Cambridge. It seems legitimate to ask whether the level of funding for pure research in a subject of such importance to so many has provided a sufficiently broad base of advanced academic inquiry to sustain the wide-ranging and intellectually robust analysis of individual and collective experiences of education in all its diversity, richness and complexity.

The other reflection is more immediate to Sheffield Hallam University. The School of Education in the 1990s and early 2000s succeeded in nurturing and developing a significant research culture of good quality. This marked a major change from the 1960s and 1970s. The new Faculty is maintaining that momentum. It is less clear how widely that research culture affects the learning and teaching of the vast majority of undergraduate and PGCE students. From 1994 to 2004 no fewer than 5,914 teachers gained their Qualified Teacher Status at Sheffield Hallam University. If the future of education depends upon an increasingly sophisticated understanding of the nature of learning and of learning and teaching strategies and methodologies, then trainee teachers should be in direct contact with academic staff who are fully conversant with, if not contributing actively to, the most rigorous research. Current funding regimes make it impossible for most institutions to achieve that objective in anything other than in a selective and periodic way.

Frontage to Ecclesall Road

One plan for redeveloping the Collegiate site in the 1990s

Student numbers and key events

Year	Student numbers in all years of Initial Teacher Training	Key events
1836		Collegiate School opened on Broomhall Park Estate
1846		Start of pupil teacher scheme
1870		Forster's Education Act created School Boards and many new schools were built in Sheffield
1891		Firth College (forerunner of Sheffield University) started a Day Training College
1902		1902 Education Act abolished School Boards and set up LEAs funded from taxes
1905	132	Sheffield City Training College formally opened on 13 October 1905 by Sir William Anson
1906		Named University of Sheffield Training College
1908	217	Renamed City of Sheffield Training College
1911	189	Collegiate Hall and Southbourne residences and extended Main Building opened by Lord Loreburn
1915	165	Requisitioned as base hospital in World War One; teaching carried on at the Wesleyan Carver Street rooms
1927	200	
1930		College acquired Oaklands; the College was managed by a university and college association, Yorkshire Board of Administration
1938	185	
1944	250	Butler's 1944 Education Act introduced 17 Area Training Organizations to organize 100 colleges nationally

National Service and post World War Two emergency training changed character of college |

Year	Number	Event
1948	348	College became a member of Sheffield University's Institute of Education, the Area Training Organisation
1955	367	Jubilee year. Quite critical HMI inspection led to many improvements
1959	415	
1961	489	Three new halls of residence were built and Collegiate Hall converted to teaching space. Start of three year route.
1963	781	1963 Robbins Report established four year BEd route
1966	999	1966 Weaver Report changed governance and name to College of Education
1970	1344	First year in which those graduating and planning to teach in Primary were required to undertake professional training
1972	1300	James Report recommended mergers of colleges and started process of contraction to match output to demand
1976	1820	Area Training Organizations abolished. Merger with Sheffield City Polytechnic. New library opened.
1981	800	Student numbers had been severely cut by government, following declining birth rate
1986	760	
1992	1327	Sheffield City Polytechnic acquired university status and became Sheffield Hallam University
1994	1382	Teacher Training Agency was established to oversee numbers and funding nationally
2004	1497	Campus invigorated by new buildings: Learning Centre extension and Heart of the Campus

Teacher training graduates, 2005

Staff and some secondary teacher training graduates, Collegiate Campus, 2005

Staff and some primary teacher training graduates, Collegiate Campus, 2005

Collegiate Campus buildings, 2005

Key to Collegiate Crescent Campus

#	Building	#	Building	#	Building	#	Building
1	Broomgrove Hall	9	Collegiate Hall	18	Montgomery House (32 Collegiate Crescent)	25	Pearson Building
2	25 Broomgrove Road	10	Faculty of Health and Wellbeing	19	Mundella House (34 Collegiate Crescent)	26	Saunders Building
3	35/37 Broomgrove Road	11	Forgers (deli and bar)	20	Nursery (23 Broomgrove Road)	27	Southbourne
4	39 Broomgrove Road	12	Herbert Wing Hall	21	Oaklands (44 Collegiate Crescent)	28	Synthetic pitches
5	43/45 Broomgrove Road	13	Main Building	22	Oak Lodge (40 Collegiate Crescent)	29	The Lodge
6	College House (36 Collegiate Crescent)	14	Marshall Hall	23	Parkholme (30 Collegiate Crescent)	30	White House
7	33 Collegiate Crescent	15	Mary Badland Lecture Theatre	24	7 Park Lane	31	Woodville Hall
8	Collegiate Crescent Learning Centre	16	Mercury House (38 Collegiate Crescent)			32	Yorkon
		17	Millers Restaurant				

Conclusions

An historical retrospect across one hundred years helps highlight recurrent themes and issues. The most obvious are the difficulty faced in planning systematically and providing physical resources which were fit for purpose. The Training College started as a very quick local response - one of the quickest in the country - to a national political initiative. Right from the start, however, the site and buildings acquired from the former Collegiate school were neither adequate nor entirely suitable for their new uses. A major building programme was put in train and the lack of science laboratory facilities was rectified. Even so, the residential and teaching accommodation remained relatively dispersed and arranged in a somewhat *adhoc* way. No sooner was the first wave of improvement completed than the College totally changed function and became a wartime hospital. After World War One the College entered the only prolonged period of stability in the history of teacher education at Collegiate. Student numbers changed only slightly and relatively limited additions or alterations were made to the buildings. Even so the College lacked an adequate gymnasium until 1938.

Once expansion began again after 1945, the teaching and residential accommodation seemed increasingly ill-matched to needs and purpose. By 1954 the facilities were extremely overcrowded and, in many respects, run down. Massive efforts from the late 1950s to the early 1970s greatly extended the College's ownership of buildings and land and transformed the student residential accommodation. But much accommodation was provided through the expedient of purchasing residential houses. Ambitious proposals to transform the site along the lower Broomgrove Road and thereby create more coherent and more usable teaching buildings came, largely, to nothing. Only a few of the projected schemes secured planning permission and funding. Once the merger occurred, the immediate pressure was not from student numbers. Debates over the best use of sites concluded with the eventual disposal of Wentworth Woodhouse and then Totley. Much of Education, its contributing parts having been dispersed after 1976, was re-assigned to the Collegiate site in the 1990s. By then the overall expansion of the Polytechnic's student numbers had begun to tell on the physical resources. Capital funding by central government fell very far short of the ambitious growth in student numbers which the polytechnics achieved.

The early 1990s again saw pressures on space and for the upgrading of teaching facilities. A radical redevelopment plan to transform the Collegiate site was drawn up in 1994 (see page 123). But other demands and opportunities, and financial constraints, prevented its implementation. Resources were available for selected major works, most notably the building of the new Learning Centre at Collegiate, the thorough refurbishment of Collegiate Hall (2001), the completion of the Heart of the Campus (2003), and the overhaul of Main Building (2005), which together marked a transformation of the main teaching facilities. The fact remains that the repair, maintenance, everyday operation, and security provision for a site with 30 buildings (plus two others nearby) are costly and inefficient. However interesting, varied and attractive, the site and its wide array of buildings are the product of historical incrementalism and have rarely in the past century conformed to a coherent plan as to current, let alone future, educational and student needs. The University since its formation has invested in the significant periodic enhancement of the Collegiate site, and ensures its continued attractiveness as a working academic environment. The University is committed to a continuing programme of significant refurbishment of buildings on the site. But there are strong arguments in favour of relocating Education in spaces which are closer together and which can be adapted more readily to purpose. The creation of the new Faculty of Development and Society has opened up opportunities for a systematic review of accommodation needs and the prospect of providing such learning and teaching accommodation in flexible and interlinked spaces.

Another recurrent theme has been the dependence of teacher education on widely fluctuating student numbers. In recent years alone the total number of first-year trainees contracted nationally by the TTA fluctuated from a low of 25,457 in 1999-2000 to a high of 37,578 in 2003-2004. The TTA's successor organisation, the TDA, began consultations with teacher training providers in the autumn of 2005 over massively reducing the number of entering trainees during the next ten years, with substantial cuts by 2008-2009. This reduction in demand results from a sharp fall in the birth-rate. During the 1980s the number of live births each year recovered from the slump experienced in the early and mid 1970s. By the early 1990s just short of 700,000 live births occurred each year in England and Wales. That number fell steadily during the 1990s to just below 600,000 a year in 2000-2002 inclusive. Current forecasts suggest that the birth rate will remain at this historically low level for the next 10 years. School enrolments have already been affected by the impact of reduced numbers born each year from 1992 onwards. By 2008 the last of the fairly large year-cohorts will have completed their compulsory schooling at age 16. All year-cohorts throughout primary and secondary to the age of 16 will have contracted by 2008 from the numbers enrolled in 2003.

This dramatic demographic shift will greatly reduce the national contract for new teacher trainees. Because Sheffield Hallam University has good quality ratings from Ofsted and because it focuses on secondary shortage subjects, it should suffer fewer reductions in new trainee numbers than other training providers may experience. The focus on shortage subjects and the proactive engagement with a range of routes into teaching have been essential to the University's flourishing as one of the country's largest ITT providers. But reductions will occur. To counter-balance them, Education in the University has a strong record of effective diversification. The long-established commitment to CPD within schools and current expertise in workforce remodelling in schools should enable Education to position itself to participate in expanding staff development for teaching and support staff in schools.

In 1902 the impulse behind improvements in secondary schooling and the introduction of national systems which spawned advances in teacher education was economic competition from overseas, especially the USA and Germany. Today much of the political commitment to education comes from the same drive to provide a highly skilled workforce which will maintain or improve Britain's economic position in an intensely competitive world market place. Yet no survey of intending teachers' motives for joining the profession reveals an imperative to contribute to national economic competitiveness as one of the prime motivating factors in trainees' choice of career. An interest in the subject and a desire to make a difference for others' benefit jostle with frustration in an existing job and a desire for job stability in motivating those changing to teaching as mature students.

Yet an economic instrumentalist view of education continues to shape policies to teacher training. In 1977, Shirley Williams, as Secretary of State for Education, wanted the teacher training curriculum *'to place greater emphasis on acquainting intending teachers with the national importance of industry and commerce and the challenges which our society as a whole must face'*. She hoped that positive preference in selecting candidates for teacher training would be given to those with *'some employment outside the world of education'* and that *'eventually the great majority of teachers'* would have experience of the world of employment outside education institutions. The concerns of the Labour government in 1977, confronted with a difficult and deteriorating economy, were wholly understandable. But it remains symptomatic of official thinking that: (a) the answer to a perceived transferable skills crisis seemed to lie in superficially 'improving' teachers' attitudes towards industry and commerce, instead of ensuring that the Education school students received was as effective and well-resourced as possible; (b) the curriculum set for teacher trainees was readily expandable; and (c) potential teachers by mere contact with a different type of employment would secure invaluable insights into the challenges facing Britain in the 1970s and beyond.

The other historical continuity involves the burden of expectations placed upon the trainees. There has always been a tension between the amount of academic subject content built into the curriculum, and its level, and the range of analysis and practitioner skills and approaches that education as a subject might require. The pressures existed in the 1900s when there were unfulfilled hopes that close co-operation might be established between the College and the University of Sheffield in the teaching of science. They became more intense from the 1950s and 1960s onward, exacerbated by the drive to raise education to a degree subject. Similar debates have recurred in the late 1990s and early 2000s over, for example, the heavy requirement in the three-year undergraduate degrees in science with QTS, in which students have to undertake advanced work in two science subjects along with their modules in education and their teaching practice in schools. In some ways, the total load upon trainees was lessened by the reduction within the syllabus of material on the history, sociology, philosophy and psychology of education, cut back in the 1990s to make way for more time spent in teaching practice.

But teaching practice, and the preparation of subject material for it, has become more complex with the step-change in ICT applications to the syllabus. Part of the research emphasis within education has been on applications of ICT, and the use of ICT in teacher education at Sheffield Hallam University has been commended. Back in 1984-1985 the average number of computers in primary schools nationally was 1.7 and in secondary schools 13.4. Twenty years later the secondary schools of South Yorkshire are about to engage with a major networked e-learning programme. Yet nationwide, a significant minority of over 40 per cent of Newly Qualified Teachers (NQTs) do not rate their preparation to use ICT in their subject teaching as good or very good. Sheffield Hallam University has sought to build on what were generally good to very good reports on ICT training in secondary in 2000. And recent Ofsted reports on primary ITT have commented favourably on the ICT resources available to trainees and the direct impact of ICT in mathematics teacher education. Yet far deeper issues remain. The objective of ITT should be to move beyond replicating what happens in the classroom and probe how the ways in which subjects are structured may be changed by developments in ICT. Yet it remains the case that relatively limited time is available for lecturing staff or trainees to work through the conceptual, pedagogic, and presentational implications of rapid advances in ICT.

The dissemination of ICT has added one element of complexity to the classroom and to preparation for it. Another example, involving inter-personal rather than technical skills, has been the integration of children with Special Educational Needs into maintained schools. In 1984 only 10 per cent of school students with SEN statements attended mainstream schools. Within 10 years, 52 per cent did so. The proportion has since stabilised at about 65 per cent. The number of children with statements has also increased considerably. This change has added a extra dimension to trainees' learning needs. A further and different element of complexity has come from the increased volume of report-writing, targeting, and league-tabling. Mature NQTs nationally report that the volume of paperwork was one of the three aspects of their new jobs which most weighed down upon them. The obvious response - slow in coming and controversial to implement - is a thorough reform of working practices in and around the classroom. The government's proposals for the wide-ranging introduction of Higher Level Teaching Assistants were designed to alleviate the burden of work on classroom teachers. Setting aside the complexities and arguments about such proposed changes to working practices, one implication of them for teacher education is clear. Classroom teachers will have to become managers of learning environments in more sophisticated ways if such workforce reforms are to have a real, as distinct from superficial, burden-sharing effect. Yet the most recently published national survey of NQTs indicates that only 43 per cent of those trained on the postgraduate route, which is the main entry into the profession, feel that their preparation for working with support staff in the classroom was good or very good. This suggests the need for yet another enhancement to training.

Yet more complexity is to be added to the school working environment through government policies to locate a range of social supports and interventions on behalf of children within the schools. Again, putting aside the practicalities of implementation and the objections naturally aroused by any major change proposal, the thrust of such planned developments is to intensify the classroom teacher's awareness of social responsibilities, child-monitoring role, and capacity to co-operate with external professionals.

Many of the main developments in teacher education over the last century resulted from step-changes in teachers' professional status. One hundred years ago only 40 per cent or so of elementary school teachers held any form of certification. By the 1950s the two-year course was deemed inadequate and in the 1960s policy-makers decided that all entering teachers in government-funded schools should eventually be formally qualified in teaching and be graduates. Since the late 1970s far more attention has been given to the professional development of in-service training and the provision of programmes in leadership and management development than had ever been the case before. Current pressures on teacher education and current expectations of the classroom teacher require a far more systematic rethink than mere incrementalism allows for. There are four areas where pressures are now unprecedented.

First, subject knowledge and understanding is more rich, varied, voluminous, and complex than ever before. In virtually all subjects taught in schools there are more academic experts living today than have worked in those subjects in the whole of previous history. Sheer expertise in every discipline is increasing at extraordinary rates. Subject teachers need both a comprehension of the extent of knowledge in their disciplines and an ability to cope with it confidently and effectively. Increasingly they need to understand and manage subject knowledge, and be capable of working with its dynamic nature.

Second, approaches to teaching and learning have been transformed since the 1970s by advances in ICT. Teachers themselves are increasingly managers of learning, engaged with children whose own expectations are shaped by visual and interactive media. Training those teachers therefore requires the integration of new technologies and new methodologies into teaching strategies and practices. This is, at present, effectively achieved in Education at Sheffield Hallam University. But many colleagues would like to do far more than the prevalent restrictions of the curriculum permit in exploring the implications of the revolution in the management and dissemination of knowledge and in probing its potential.

Third, classroom management has become more demanding. In national surveys of mature NQTs, one of the three most challenging aspects of teaching as a job is the culture shock of students' behaviour and language in school. Added to this challenge is the rapidly growing sophistication of our understanding of Special Educational Needs and issues arising from multiculturalism. The range of aptitudes and skills required for managing classroom groups and responding effectively is clearly different from those needed to manage knowledge and those needed to manage learning. For many trainees, human interaction and the desire to make a difference socially and in personal terms impels them into the profession. Coping with some of the behavioural realities in some schools becomes disillusioning as well as problematic. If, as the TTA argued in 2003, teacher retention rather than teacher recruitment is the main concern over the profession's future, then this is an aspect of teacher training which requires considerable further development. Of course, classroom management is not a new issue. Some trainees of the 1970s have pointed out that, while their academic preparation was stimulating and effective, they did not feel well prepared for the experience of the secondary classroom. Shifting the focus of postgraduate teacher education increasingly to in-school practice does not seem to have overcome such reported shortcomings. National surveys of NQTs - and Sheffield Hallam University's returns are in line with those national responses - continue to report that one of the three aspects of their training which seemed least adequate in preparing them for their teaching jobs is classroom management. Existing training schemes and the school induction year are clearly not giving satisfactory levels of support in this area to a significant minority of trainees.

Fourth, one partial solution to the weight of demands on classroom teaching is the government's workforce reform agenda. This will in turn create new challenges of team-building and co-ordination which do not always come naturally in busy situations where there are high levels of intense personal interaction. So, too, participating in and acting upon an increasing range of external professional interventions concerning childrens' welfare and behaviour will create issues around legal responsibility, individual rights and duties, and boundary definitions between and within agencies and schools which require further training for teachers.

These pressures are not individually new, but they have each become increasingly complex and demanding in the last decade or so. To many of these challenges government, the profession, and the teacher education providers have responded with an increasing provision of CPD programmes and initiatives. But the perspective of a brief history of one provider of teacher education suggests that a further step-change is needed either to extend the length of time devoted to full-time ITT or to provide a structured, sequential, and accredited programme of in-service training for four or five years beyond QTS, preferably to a formal qualification such as a Masters degree.

The James Report of 1972 concluded that pre-service education and training and the teachers' probationary year were together *'no more than a foundation'* for future developments in the profession and teachers' individual careers. This theme was picked up in the White Paper of 1977, *'Education in Schools: A Consultative Document'*, which endorsed the view that *'a coherent approach is needed in which policies for the initial education and training of teachers, induction, in-service training, and other aspects of the deployment and career development of the teachers will combine to provide staff for schools better equipped to deal with their present and emergent tasks'*. A major increase in in-service training followed, but no systematic framework was embedded.

The issue re-emerged when part of the remit of the General Teaching Council established in 2000 was to press for more coherent programmes of staff development. But the real breakthrough is promised with the creation in 2005 of the Training and Development Agency for schools. One of the TDA's four strategic aims is to *'enable schools to develop the effectiveness of their teachers and keep their knowledge and skills up to date'*. A new framework for teachers' CPD and new standards for teachers, usable in staff training programmes supported by development work, should be forthcoming in 2006. Complementing this objective is the further strategic aim to support schools in the effective management of *'the training, development and remodelling of their workforce'*.

We remain nationally some way from offering full professional training for practising teachers. As was the case one hundred years ago, teacher education nationally often appears to be striving to keep up with developments in schools and pressures from the larger society which are well beyond teachers' and teacher trainers' control. But Sheffield Hallam University's proactive engagement over the last three decades with the full range of approaches to initial teacher education, and with consultancy, research and staff development within schools, provides teacher education at the University with a strong base from which to play a creative role in the future.

Sheffield City Training College/Sheffield City Polytechnic/Sheffield Hallam University: actual teacher training student numbers at five year intervals

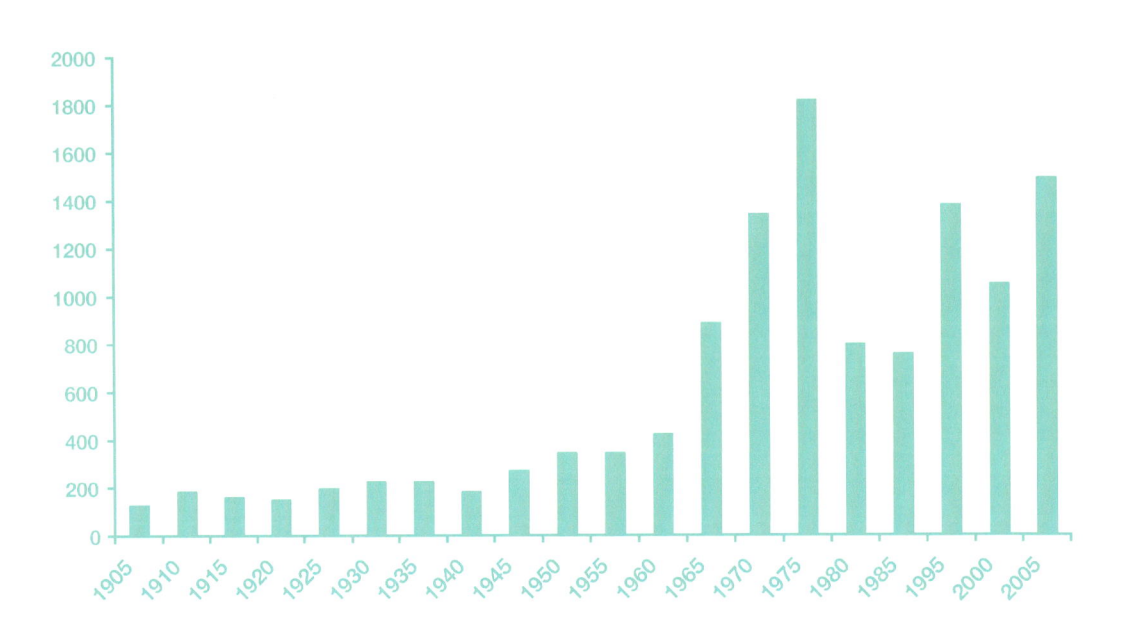

References and further reading

This book is designed for a readership interested in the history of teacher education at the College/Polytechnic/University. It is not a contribution to scholarship, but synthesises information and insight about the institution and key themes and issues in the development of teacher education both locally and nationally. We have drawn widely on the research and interpretations of others. The main sources of our reading are listed here. The nature of this publication means that we have not been able to include footnotes and detailed references. Our debt to others' work will be apparent to scholars in the field.

Alexander RJ, Craft M and Lynch J (1984) *Change in Teacher Education, Context and Provision since Robbins.* Holt, Rinehart and Winston.

Bagley JJ and AJ (1969) *The State and Education in England and Wales 1833-1968.* St Martins.

Bambery A (1981) *Walk around Broomhall Estate.* Victorian Society.

Bayn B Newspaper cuttings relating to Stainless Stephen 1932-95

City of Sheffield Education Committee Minutes and Reports

City of Sheffield Archives (CA523 -21) Papers of City College Governing Body 1963-69

Coldwell M et al (2003) *Charter for Transition.* Final Evaluation Report for Barnsley LEA/SRB3.

Collegiate Magazine 1852

Crescent Magazine for 1905-1908, 1914-1916, 1936-1942, 1946-1947, 1951-1968.

Dent HC (1970) 1870-1970 *Century of Growth in English Education.* Longman.

Dent HC (1977) *The Training of Teachers in England and Wales 1800-1975.* Hodder and Stoughton.

DfE *Statistical Bulletin* 14/94 (August 1994); 17/94 (November 1994)

DfE *Circular* No. 14/93 (23 November 1993)

DfES (2001) *Education and Training Statistics for the United Kingdom, 2001 edition.*

Education 2 March 1973; 11 January 1974; 22 November, 20/27 December 1991; 8 December 1995; 5/19/26 January, 9 February 1996.

Education in Schools. A Consultative Document. Cmnd 6869 July 1977.

Furlong J and Smith R (1996) *The Role of Higher Education in Initial Teacher Training.* Kogan Page.

Gasden P (1990) The James Report and Recent History. In Thomas JB (ed) *British Universities and Teacher Education, A Century of Change.* Falmer 73-86.

Gatty A (1873) *Sheffield: Past and Present.* Thomas Rodgers, Sheffield.

General Teaching Council, *Annual Reports.*

Harman R and Minnis J (2004) *Sheffield.* Pevsner Architectural Guides, Yale University Press

HEFCE et al (1996) *Research Assessment Exercise, The Outcome.*

HEFCE et al (2001) *Research Assessment Exercise, The Outcome.*

History of Hadfield, Cawkwell and Davidson 1834-1976

Hunter J (c1870) *Hallamshire.* Virtue and Co Ltd, London.

Jacob GA (1852) *Sheffield Collegiate School.* Simpkin, Marshall and Co, London.

Jones LGE (1924) *The Training of Teachers in England and Wales - A Critical Survey.* OUP.

Levi P (1993) *Tennyson.* MacMillan.

Lofthouse A (2001) *Then and Now - the Sheffield Blitz.* Northern Map Distributors.

Maclure S (2000) *The Inspector Calling: HMI and the Shaping of Education Policy 1945-1992*

Mathers H (2005) *Steel City Scholars, the Centenary History of the University of Sheffield.* James and James.

Millington R (1955) *A History of the City of Sheffield Training College.* Sheffield City Training College public.

Odom Rev W (1926) *Hallamshire Worthies.* Northends.

Ofsted (1994) Report on Secondary Initial Teacher Training Courses, Sheffield Hallam University, June and Oct 1993. 91/94/HE.

Oldfield B (2004) *Rootless* Arrow

Pawson and Brailsford (1971) *Illustrated Guide to Sheffield.* SR Publishers Ltd.

Park A et al (2003) *British Social Attitudes.* The 20th Report.

Peake HJ (1970) *Sheffield City College - A Five Year Review*

Priyadharsini E and Robinson-Pant A (2003) The Attractions of Teaching: an investigation into why people change careers to teach. *Journal of Education for Teaching* 29 95-112.

Report of Committee of Council on Education 1898/99

Rich RW (1933) *The training of teachers in England and Wales in the Nineteenth-century.*

Ross A (1990) The Universities and the BEd degree. In Thomas JB (ed) *British Universities and Teacher Education, A Century of Change.* Falmer 58-72.

Sandiford P (1910) *The Training of teachers in England and Wales.* Columbia NY.

Shakoor A (1964) *The Training of Teachers in England and Wales 1900-1939.* PhD thesis, University of Leicester.

Sheffield City Polytechnic Annual Reports for 1986/87, 1987/88, 1988/89 and 1991/92.

Simon B (1990) The Study of Education as a University Subject. In Thomas JB (ed) *British Universities and Teacher Education, A Century of Change.* Falmer 125-142.

Stainton JH (1924) *The Making of Sheffield 1865-1914.* E Weston and Sons, Sheffield.

Taylor L (2004) How Student Teachers Develop their Understanding of Teaching using ICT. *Journal of Education for Teaching* 30 43-56.

Thomas JB (1990) Victorian Beginnings. In Thomas JB (ed) *British Universities and Teacher Education, A Century of Change.* Falmer 125-142.

Times Higher Education Supplement 18 January, 2 August, 27 September 1974.

Tropp A (1957) *The School Teachers. The growth of the teaching profession in England and Wales from 1800 to the present day.* Heinemann.

TTA website: *Initial Teacher Training: Performance Profiles.*

TTA website: *Results of the Newly Qualified Teacher Survey 2005.*

Turner JD (1990) The Area Training Organisation. In Thomas JB (ed) *British Universities and Teacher Education, A Century of Change.* Falmer 39-57.

Watson A and de Geest E (2005) Principled Teaching for Deep Progress: Improving Mathematical Learning beyond Methods and Materials. *Educational Studies in Mathematics* 58 209-234.

Wheelan S and Kesselring J (2005) Link between Faculty Group Development and Elementary Student Performance on Standardized Tests. *Journal of Educational Research* 98 323-330.

Wilson N (1999) *The Development of Middle-Class Housing in Western Sheffield during the 19th Century.* PhD thesis University of Sheffield.

Glossary

ATCDE	Association of Teachers in Colleges and Departments of Education
CNAA	Council for National Academic Awards
CPD	Continuing Professional Development
DfES	Department for Education and Skills
GTP	Graduate Teacher Programme
HE	Higher Education
HMI	Her Majesty's Inspector
ICT	Information and Communications Technology
ITT	Initial Teacher Training
LEA	Local Education Authority
NQT	Newly Qualified Teacher
PGCE	Postgraduate Certificate in Education
QTS	Qualified Teacher Status
RAE	Research Assessment Exercise
SYeLP	South Yorkshire e-Learning Programme
TDA	Training and Development Agency for Schools (replacing TTA in 2005)
TESOL	Teaching of English to Speakers of Other Languages
TTA	Teacher Training Agency